I Don't BRAKE for Nuns

A kid-turned-adult perspective of Catholic School and the nun-run classroom in the 1960s

Sister liked to swat kids with her ruler so she could measure a kid's wounds at the same time.

Rick Phillips

ISBN: 1-4505-9607-X
ISBN-13: 9781450596077

ACKNOWLEDGMENT

I've been inspired by many people over the years to write a book about my grade school experiences, due in great part to my penchant for anecdotal exaggeration.

Thanks to my wife, Camille, for her encouragement and her great humor to propel me forward in this project. My special thanks to my lifelong best friend, Dan Volpendesta, whose Mensa-like memory helped me keep my anecdotes, ideas, and humor on track for all these decades.

My appreciation to Stan Pakowitz, who has helped me hone my sense of comedy for years, and was instrumental in my improving this book's humor.

I'm also grateful to my sister Darlene, who has given me great encouragement, and has inspired me to make others laugh. A special thanks to my brother Bud, who read this manuscript first and gave it a thumbs up. He provided me with invaluable advice for its final writing.

I'm also grateful to Michelle Slagel, Stanley Rosenthal, Candy Rechtschaffer, Maryanne

Young, and all those who've laughed and suggested that I write this book.

Finally, thanks to my fellow pupils at Immaculate Conception for being the best group of kids with whom to grow up. And to the teachers (and nuns!) for providing us all with an excellent, disciplined education (psychological scars notwithstanding!).

CONTENTS

FOREWORD

There are two types of adults in this world, as far as I can distinguish. Those who went to Catholic School, and those who are glad they didn't. This book is to be enjoyed by both types of people.

The narrative "I DON'T BRAKE FOR NUNS!" is a serious, tongue-in-cheek, precise exaggeration that enables readers to put themselves back at their desk and relive for themselves their own school days. This book appeals to everyone who always wanted to go back to those days of yesteryear with an adult mind, and alter the course of classroom history.

Every student—young or old—can remember vividly the tyranny of the grade school classroom. Only a refugee of Catholic school, however, can extract so much humor out of such a restrictive and punitive experience.

The ones who went to Catholic School and endured the tyrant-like tirades of the nuns will identify with the experiences and observances depicted in this book. Folks who never went to

Catholic School certainly have heard the stories about the parochial-style teaching methods employed by the nuns. Those who casually cruised through public school may come to think of Catholic School more like walking the plank of a pirate's ship.

The book begins by comically explaining the prison-like reputation of Immaculate Conception School and the ignominious image of its nuns. We laugh at each nun's personality characteristics, and the conflicts that arise between indentured students and the diabolical Sisters of Loretto. "I DON'T BRAKE FOR NUNS!" delineates the day-to-day struggles that students encounter under the hyper-scrutiny of the nuns, all while being molded by a Catholic-style education.

From the pugilistic prowess of the nuns to the joys of recess, the book reminds its readers how comical it was to be young, innocent and over-disciplined by psychopathic convent-dwellers. The book explores the "Catholic Guilt" treatment, and the anti-social relationships between students and teachers.

"I DON'T BRAKE FOR NUNS!" also describes the student's point of view of the religion and the hypocrisy, showing that even children are perspicacious enough to understand the complexity of a Catholic-style education. In the end, it's discovered that some human traits can be attributed to the nuns, after all.

Maybe it was all a facade. Maybe nuns are just like people. Maybe they really are sensitive, caring individuals deep down inside. Maybe they really DO care about kids...Nah!

Oh, there are some who will say Catholic School wasn't anything like that. The nuns were wonderful, and the experience was a delight. They may be right. Perhaps not every Catholic School was run like Joliet Prison.

I'm sure you could find prisoners of war who would say that their incarceration was like a holiday in the Bavarian Forest. Or the Hanoi Hilton was really a Southeast Asian-style Club Med. I suggest that you think of these people as extraordinary, and their view of Catholic School as slightly out of focus.

"I DON'T BRAKE FOR NUNS!" is a look at Catholic School in the 1960s through the eyes of a kid stuck right smack in the middle of a nun-run educational system. If you've never experienced an encounter with a nun, you have no idea what six hours a day with one can be like. This book will help shine a light on what that experience might be like.

I always felt Don Rickles would have made a great nun. He had all the natural qualities that a dynamic nun possesses. He had the innate ability to stand up in front of an audience and, one at a time, pick out individuals to berate. Nuns do it all the time. Rickles can abuse someone with personal insults and make the rest of the audience laugh. So can nuns. Rickles could walk around a room and have each person hold his breath, afraid of being singled out with an onslaught of mockery and derision.

Nuns have been doing Rickles' routine for generations. All Rickles would have to do is learn to slap, tweak, pinch, chop and gouge, and his repertoire would be complete for nunhood. Of course, there would be the problem of converting to Catholicism, and becoming neutered.

There are still some people out there afraid to admit that the nuns were lunatics, somehow fearing that they may be thrust back into time, forced to endure the wrath of a nun's retribution.

Well, I'm not afraid. Not any more, I'm not. Take a look around you. How many nuns do you see on the loose? Most of the truly dangerous ones have been rounded up by the authorities, or the militia, or vigilantes, quietly in the night, and whisked away, I suspect, to some home for wayward nuns.

Nuns are on the endangered species list now, and many former Catholic School kids like me rejoice in that fact. I say hallelujah! Those who survived Catholic School have a special bond with each other, and it was the nuns that served as the glue. We look back on our school days fondly, knowing that we suffered and endured proudly, in true Catholic fashion. Catholics admire nothing more than one's tolerance to pain and suffering. Being able to laugh about it later is what makes it so worthwhile.

THE IGNOMINY
OF IMMACULATE
CONCEPTION

I remember one day staring out the window, fixated on a spot that was still clear of condensation, allowing me a tiny porthole of a view to the outside world. It was still drizzling, an endless precipitation that only added to the dreary setting of misery going on inside the classroom.

Sister Agnes Marita droned on in her usual dictatorial drivel as I imagined the pleasure of standing in the cold rain, hitchhiking a ride, taking me far, far away from the captivity of that fifth-grade classroom.

Buttressing my enormously heavy head from full collapse onto my desk, I watched the cars across the street splash their way to their destinations. I imagined the motorists looking over at the school, laughing at my incarceration.

It was laughable, even cruelly ironic to the captured students inside, that the road running alongside my classroom was called Pleasant Avenue. Peasant Avenue would have been more accurate, for surely we were indentured by these manorial nuns.

As the cars whizzed by, I could almost hear mothers in their cars warning their kids that they'd better behave lest they be sent off to the Catholic School. The scare tactic was far more pernicious to a kid than, say, threatening to tell Santa Claus of one's yearlong misbehavior. Missing a few presents at Christmas time could be endured. Day after day of Immaculate Conception was a sentence tantamount to being conscripted to a chain gang.

"There's where I'll send you next time you don't make your bed," the mother says. "Immaculate Conception. A few years of schooling there will wipe that smirk off your face, young man."

Kids who didn't go to I.C. didn't even like to look over at the infamous, red-bricked building. They knew that kids their own age were paying a dear price with their youth by being forced to attend that parochial school.

Other kids basically blocked Immaculate Conception out of their minds. It's kind of like how old people don't look at cemeteries when they drive by one. They know it's there. And they know how you get entrance there, too. They just try not to dwell on it.

Nobody ever made fun of I.C. kids just because they went to school there. It was like having people feeling sorry for you more than anything else. Around town, I.C. kids were treated by their peers as if they were cross-eyed. They were hard to look in the face at first, but then, after a while, it wasn't that noticeable.

The meaning of Immaculate Conception is pretty much a mystery to most people, especially Catholics. It doesn't mean that Mary, the Mother of Jesus, was a virgin, although the notion that the Virgin Mary could possibly be anything else but a virgin is beyond reproach to the staunch Catholics. Indeed, Jesus was born to Mary as would any child be born, only the supernatural influence of the Holy Ghost replaced Joseph's contribution to the conception. Most students that I knew at I.C. left the school without even knowing exactly what "Immaculate Conception" meant.

The simple two words of "Immaculate Conception" means Mary, the Mother of Jesus, was herself born with purity—that is, without Original Sin. Naturally, these declarations are made by men who sat in councils hundreds of years ago.

So, rather than blurt out Immaculate Conception at every reference, the school became widely known as I.C. We, the indentured ones, had our own spellout of the initials I.C. In Chains. InCompetence. Innocent Children. Irrational Catholics.

The question "Where do you go to school?" is invariably answered with resignation and a sullen muffling, "I.C." I don't know why everybody then repeats what you just said, questioning their own hearing. "I.C.? You go to I.C.?"

I always answered this same, follow-up question with emphasis. "YES! I go to I.C. And I can prove it, too! You want to see the bumps on my head? Here, feel these bumps."

I would stick my head under the inquisitor's nose and show him my scalp up close.

It was well understood that bumps on the head came courtesy of the ruler-wielding nuns. I never knew anyone who actually received a bump on the head from a nun, however. But the rest of the world was convinced that there were plenty of concussions going on inside those holy walls. How naive. There was a lot of mental scarring going on. Permanent psychological damage, to be sure. But signs of physical injuries were rare.

The nuns were professionals. They didn't leave bumps on heads for all to see. They slapped with open hands, pulled hair, slugged backs, tweaked ears, squeezed cheeks, clawed necks, yanked arms, and bullied kids all over the place, often times at the drop of a hat.

You never knew when you were going to get accosted or caught up in a nun's tirade. It was usually when you least expected it. Surprise was a nun's number-one assault tactic.

That's why if you were going to survive Catholic School, you had better be paying attention. At all times. Just daydreaming was cause enough for a nun to sneak up behind you and lower the boom on your head with a book.

In all my years at I.C., that's from kindergarten to 8th grade graduation, I never saw a kid successfully duck a nun's attack.

For example. John Lorrenzo was a brilliant student and a well behaved one, too, in seventh grade. Yet it didn't save him from having Sister Daniel Marie sucker slap him with a left that came out of nowhere. He never saw it coming. Didn't even have a chance to roll a bit with the biff. Neither did he have a chance to take his glasses off. He took it full on the face, sending his black-framed goggles hurtling across the room.

That was one of the dangers of being around a nun on a rampage. Not only could you get smacked for nothing. You also could get hit by flying debris. Collateral injuries were very possible. Lorrenzo's glasses just missed Richard Coffet's head as they flew onto Daphne Dohring's desk then onto the floor and under the radiator, some thirty feet away from Lorrenzo's red, right cheek.

In the streets, there was always the fighting axiom, you don't hit a guy with glasses on. But the halls of Immaculate Conception weren't the streets, baby. It wasn't even the alley. Getting belted with glasses on was mere child's play for the nuns. These crazed psychopaths would kick the crutches out from under a kid with polio if she caught him talking in line, for chrissake.

You'd better have your hands on top of your desk when a nun gets a head of steam rolling. I got my fingers bashed between my desk and the kid's chair ahead of me when Sister Agnes Marita crashed through the aisle like a rhinoceros. She was about to tear Ray Gracie's arm from his socket for waving it in the air a bit too demonstratively to answer a question. Sometimes a kid tries too hard to get on a nun's good side. Gracie figured, answering lots of questions by raising his hand with an "Ooh, ooh, sister, I know, I know..." was a favorable approach. That day when I got my fingernails squashed, he found out differently.

Gracie's arm wrenching was just another interesting torture technique. The nuns have a complete repertoire of punishment methods. Over the years, I watched some sixty kids, including myself, get belted one way or another a thousand times. I never once saw a nun repeat the exact same technique.

I never understood how these nuns got so good at slapping and attacking. They were like martial artists, trained in hand-to-hand combat. They were downright clever about it, too. It wasn't always a slap. Sometimes it was a grab. Maybe a poke. A chop. A tweak.

That's why I never saw a kid block a slap, avoid a hair pull, or dodge a neck wrenching. The nuns were obviously highly trained legerdomainists. I imagine they had a speed bag hanging in the convent up on the hill. Perhaps a few punching bags. Maybe they sparred with each other in a ring after school. More likely, they practiced the same beatings they received when they were kids, either from their parents or from other nuns. All I know is, they were good.

I remember thinking when Floyd Patterson was heavyweight champion what little chance he'd have with some of I.C.'s nuns. Patterson used to have a patented, peek-a-boo stance, peering over his gloves covering his face. Each kid at I.C. had that same stance when a nun went into her whirling-dervish flurry of slaps and chops. All you could do was cover-up and peek to see when the coast was clear.

When a nun locked in on you, and decided you were in for a whooping, there was no changing her course. If a nun had it in for you on a particular day, you knew your number was up. Not even a call from the governor could get you out of it.

Generally though, if you kept your head up and on a swivel, you weren't likely to get cold-cocked by surprise.

The main entrance of Immaculate Conception. The original building remains, but the cries of suffering Catholic kids has long been quieted.

LONG LIVE
BAZOOKA JOE

One thing you didn't want to do is look in any way, shape or form like you were chewing gum. Nothing begs a nun's rage like a kid chewing gum. You don't even want to look like you're chewing gum. It's immaterial whether you are or not.

There's something inherently evil about gum to a nun. It's kind of like how a mouse will drive an elephant crazy. Maybe gum gets caught on their heels or stuck on their rosary beads, or something. I've always wondered if Wrigley's and the Catholic Church were ever at war...or if the nuns just hated the likes of Bazooka Joe and his pals.

One day, Sister Daniel Marie descended on David Pasqualoni for allegedly chewing gum. She simply snuck up on him, grabbed him under the chin and forced his jaw to open wide.

"Are you chewing gum? Huh! Well, are you?" she demanded.

All Pasqualoni could do with the nun's fingers in his mouth was gargle out an "uhng-uh." As the nun continued to inspect his tonsils for signs of gum, Pasqualoni's head bobbed and swung around like a tuna trying to fight his way off a fisherman's hook.

"Where's the gum?" she shouted to the seventh grader who was still trying to get feeling back into his jaw.

"I'm not chewing gum," he mumbled.

"Then stop chewing your cud," she demanded, and continued on with her class.

Every I.C. kid knew there was a nun's manual somewhere that explained how to extricate oneself from an incorrect assessment of guilt. Blaming Pasqualoni for chewing his cud like a cow was an easy way out for a nun desperately trying to catch a kid chewing gum.

The nuns tried so hard to find a kid chewing gum that it was scary to think what they would have done had a kid actually been caught red handed, or red tongued. Must have been some punishment comparable to a trip up Cavalry Hill, if not full crucifixion.

In nine years, I never saw a kid chewing gum at Immaculate Conception. Never saw the gummy substance anywhere. Except under the pews at church.

I think the nuns would get wind of gum being stuck under a desk in their classroom. Maybe the janitor would say something like, "Hey, sister, I'm sorry for bothering you, but I know you'll be interested to know that I found a wad of bubble gum under desk four, row three."

The nuns weren't judicious enough to realize that the gum may have been put there by some other tenant of Pasqualoni's desk. Would a nun perhaps suspect that the CCD crowd that took night classes in religious studies in that very room were guilty? No, no, no. It was the student who was guilty. All the evidence was there. Pasqualoni's desk had gum underneath it, ergo, Pasqualoni is chewing gum in class.

That's the kind of tip a nun would pay kickback money for. It was a chance to capture a kid in a guilty situation and humiliate him with all sorts of theatrics. I'm sure the nuns stayed up at night contemplating their next day's assaults.

Immaculate Conception certainly was a house of detention all right. Kids from 5 to 14 who have never done a crime were brought there. Some by their parents, others by bus, some even walked from nearby neighborhoods. The sign on the red brick wall at the front entrance read "Immaculate Conception Catholic School, Kindergarten through 8th Grade."

To the prisoners inside, however, it was a gulag run by nuns the way prison guards rule a block house in the state prison.

Oh, parents thought they were doing their kids a favor for life: good education, discipline, ethics, religious upbringing. What went on inside, day to day, wasn't exactly what the parents thought.

What was the difference between this place and San Quentin? That would have been an interesting essay. Immaculate Conception's strict reputation was well known in this region of Chicago. Maybe the world for all I knew.

Hmm. Nuns as hood ornaments...Not a bad idea in the 1960's.

YOUR DESK IS YOUR LIFE RAFT

Every desk was the same in school. Uniqueness wasn't tolerated in any form at Immaculate Conception. You didn't want to stand out or draw attention to yourself here. Not even if you were a desk. The chairs conformed, too, matching the desk, sliding underneath perfectly when neatly arranged, showing only the tippy top of the backrest and its cut-out handle.

It would be impossible to find your desk when entering a classroom since they all looked the same. You memorized your row and seat.

Some schools have pupils moving from room to room, depending on the class or subject matter. Not so at Immaculate Conception. The kids stayed put. You barely moved all day long. Your desk was YOUR desk.

Your desk was a metaphor for a lot of things. In a way, it was like your own, personal life raft. Everything you needed to survive Catholic School was under the wooden lid, inside that mini-sar-cophagus. The desk was also your jail cell. You might as well have been surrounded by invisible bars or handcuffed to the desk, since getting up and moving around wasn't encouraged. Your desk was susceptible to shakedowns, too, without warning.

Nuns liked to go on clandestine desk inspec-tions, discovering all they could about a kid and his habits. One's hygiene could be determined by the neatness of his or her desk. One was a slob if the books weren't aligned in perfect order and ac-cording to height. A messy desk surely would sub-ject a student to public ridicule. The nun would find a way to get revenge on a kid who stepped out of line at some time. There certainly was a log somewhere that chronicled every indiscretion a kid made in school. Sooner or later, he'd pay for it. The messy desk was just one of an arsenal of weapons the nuns used to inflict mental wounds and punishment.

It wasn't inconceivable that your desk could look like a mess at times. Nuns were handing back your homework all the time. Papers mounted up. You had your loose leaf folder strewn among your reading workbook, religious text, speller, diction-ary, history book, English book, and music book.

Your scissors hangs through the inexplicable holes in the desk. You don't know why, but that's what everyone else did with them. Pencils, pens, tacks and paper clips are strewn in the tray just beneath your ruler. Your gummy eraser bounces out of the tray most of the time, lodging God knows where. If you drop your eraser, it will bounce and tumble its way into another aisle of desks, perhaps lost forever, since getting out of your seat to retrieve it is too risky a venture in a nun's classroom.

Nuns don't like kids getting out of their seat. They think of it as the first step of rebellion. The smart play would be to leave the eraser there the entire day until you can pick it up after school.

Sometimes, a pal will notice the escaped eraser and try to help you out. If he can reach it while pretending to pull up his sock, you're in luck. If bending over is too risky, a sort of golf-putting game ensues. He'll line up the eraser with your foot and try to putt it across the aisle to you without being noticed. The key to not drawing attention is to keep your head up, looking forward, exactly the opposite of keeping your head down in golf. With the right bounce of the eraser, you can block the putt with your own foot, then casually slink down in your chair and capture the eraser while lifting the lid of your desk, thus concealing your slouching.

This, of course, is considering you don't sit in the first row. Kids sitting in the first row are absolutely proscribed from doing any chicanery. It's simply too risky.

Passing notes is in the Top 10 of worst crimes possible in Catholic School. Punishment varies. I saw Sister Agnes Marita drag Marsha Nolan by her ponytail to the front of the class and told to read the note out loud to the class. The teary fifth-grader read: "Can I borrow—"

The nun questioned Marsha what the note was asking for. The kid said sobbing, "I ran out of paper."

The nun continued her righteous harangue by reminding the whole class how important it was to come to class prepared. The whole class, she explained, can't be disrupted every time Marsha Nolan needs paper!

I always wondered how quietly passing a note asking for a sheet of paper was disrupting the class. Certainly it wasn't as disruptive as the five-minute public humiliation and hair pulling that ensued.

But that's the way the nuns taught. You didn't learn as much about your subjects—Math,

English, History— as you did about tolerance of disgrace and humiliation.

It was all about fear, which the nuns used as their number-one teaching instrument. And they were right. Fear is a great pedagogical motivator. Many dictators proved the same tactic is very effective in keeping insurgencies to a minimum. The difference is, nuns teach children; dictators quell bloody revolutions.

LEARNING STEALTH WITH FRITOS

At Immaculate Conception, only one teacher presided over the class the entire day. A student had the pleasure of looking at the same figure at the front of the room all day, every day from 8:30 a.m. to 2:45 p.m.

Most nuns soliloquized at the front of the room, with perfect diction, morning, noon and afternoon long. It mostly was like watching Mussolini all day blabbering on from a balcony.

Kids got called on to punctuate the nun's lecture, mostly so the nun could come up for air. But more importantly, the nun would take an amusing break from her dissertation to catch some kid daydreaming off somewhere in the twilight zone.

Most kids would find themselves drifting away from time to time, searching for nirvana, as the nun droned on about linking verbs and predicate adjectives, or filibustered over the righteousness of the Crusades. Sometimes, it was as if there were a time warp in the classroom. The clock on the wall with its imperceptibly moving second hand would give cause for double take. One minute it appears to be 10:35, the next minute it was 10:32.

A nun's lecture could make time stand still. Or even run backwards. The only thing that kept some kids from outright falling out of their chairs with boredom was the nun's occasional drifting between the rows of desks, surveying the students, keeping their attention by peering into their eye-weary faces.

Sister Agnes Marita was particularly effective in holding kids' attention during her filibusters. She'd walk down the aisle peering into kids' faces, almost questioning whether they were still alive. When she got to the back of the classroom, still jabbering on, she'd linger, making you wonder which row she would choose to return to the front. Since it was taboo to turn around, only your ears could ascertain the direction of the shifty nun. You never wanted to be inattentive at this point. It was far too dangerous not to know where a nun was at all times. Most nuns were like cobras. As soon as you got careless, they were bound to strike. It was always great relief to realize she was choosing someone else's row to carouse. When a nun chose to go on her occasional classroom promenades, you had better be sure you had any contraband put away securely and out of sight, sound or smell. It was well known that nuns had souped-up olfactory glands that could smell an open bag of Fritos from six rows away.

It was common practice for a kid to surreptitiously sneak a few Fritos from his lunch bag for a pre-lunch munch. This clandestine, classroom appetizer, of course, took raw courage. It was impossible for a kid to dispatch Fritos from his lunch bag, slip the chips under his desk lid, and then into his mouth without his surrounding classmate neighbors being on to him. (The nuns referred to kids sitting around you as your "neighbors." E.G. "Hand your paper to your neighbor." "Stop visiting with your neighbors.")

The technique of eating Fritos during class was classic. First, you deftly extricated a few corn chips from your lunch bag without making any paper-crackling noise. The small, lunch-size Fritos bags were easily opened with a simple tear that made no noise. Kids today are grateful to the Fritolay folks for the courtesy of making noiseless Fritos bags.

You load a few chips in your pencil tray, which runs the width of the front of your desk. Now, you can nonchalantly open the lid of your desk half an inch and grab a chip with your index and middle fingers while holding the desk lid open with your thumb. While pulling a chip from your desk, it's advisable to do a "look-off." That is, look at something at a 35-degree angle as you're pulling out the chip. If a nun happens to see you, her scrutiny will be taken away from your desk. Instinctively, she'll look for whatever is distracting you. Usually, she'll figure another one of your classmates is fooling around, and she'll focus on him or her while you work the Fritos into your mouth.

The tricky part here is to not let the corn chip ever be seen. You do a sort of palming of the chip, like a magician hiding a quarter. Now, you rub your face or your eye while slipping the Frito into your pie hole. Once you have the Frito in your mouth, you treat it as if you've just received communion. You don't bite or chew, ever. You suck it for five minutes until it dissolves away.

Of course, you never want it to appear as if you're chewing gum, thereby breaking the nuns'

Eleventh Commandment, "Though shall not chew gum or imitate the act of chewing gum."

It's also important to remember that the smell of Fritos outlasts the actual chip itself. Long after you've swallowed it, the Frito continues to send out wafts of its undeniably distinct scent.

If a nun comes down your aisle and calls on you after you've been sucking on Fritos, there are a couple of things you can do. Either look stunned at the question, silently searching your mind for the answer, or, answer like Edgar Bergen, ventriloquist-style. Whichever you choose, you must keep your mouth shut! Opening your mouth after Frito munching is way too perilous a risk. The Fritos smell will travel from your tongue to the nun's nostrils at the speed of sound, thus sentencing you to a sure slapping.

Jeff Ralston was sucking down a few Fritos one morning when Sister Ann Bernadette decided to take a stroll down his aisle. I saw him freeze up with fear. His jaw tightened up and his eyes bugged out as the nun approached his desk. She wasn't on to him until she saw that deer-in-the-headlights look on his face. So she sent a trial balloon up to see what Ralston was up to.

"Jeffrey, how do you think the Grand Canyon was formed?"

Ralston chose the wrong response. He simply shrugged with a dumb look on his face.

Everyone knows that nuns never buy a shrug. It only leads to another question.

"Don't shrug your shoulders. Can't you answer? What have you got in your mouth?"

Ralston's eyebrows reached the top of his head as he realized the nun was coming at him full-steam ahead to inspect his yapper.

"ARE YOU CHEWING GUM!"

Ralston shook his head violently in denial as he tried to gulp down the contraband in his mouth. But he wasn't quick enough. Sister Ann Bernadette grabbed him by the chin with one hand and his forehead with the other and opened his mouth like a giant clam. Ralston's tongue was loaded with ground-up Fritos.

Caught red-handed, Ralston was at the nun's mercy, which was a pretty hopeless place to be. He made several mistakes. First he panicked, then he shrugged, but worst of all, he got greedy by jamming a fistful of Fritos in his trap all at once.

The berserk nun went on a hair pulling rage, giving Ralston's neck and scalp a workout.

"Don't you get enough to eat at home?" the old wench asked rhetorically. "You think my class is a lunchroom?"

Ralston simply went limp and into that same anesthesia that a springbok goes into before it's devoured by a lion. Sister Ann Bernadette opens up his desk and yanks out his lunch bag, spilling the remainder of Fritos on the floor.

"Pick those up," she demanded of Ralston, as she headed back to the front of the class holding her confiscated lunch bag prize. "Now, Jeffrey, since you've already had YOUR lunch, you can remain seated when the class dismisses for the cafeteria."

The bellicose nun then tossed his brown lunch bag halfway across the room into the large, brown, metal trash can that sat in the corner, just as an exact duplicate can does in every I.C. classroom.

Ralston finally scooped up the remaining Fritos strewn on the floor by the rampaging nun, and stood in the aisle dumbfounded with a handful of crumbs, looking around for divine intervention. The nun's ire continued.

"Don't just stand there, big boy! Bring that mess up here!" Ralston crept up to her sheepishly with his handful of corn crumbs extended as an offering, or something.

"Put it in the bin!" she hollered, while thrusting her arm violently while pointing to the innocent trash can.

Ralston dropped the chip remains into the can, then clapped his hands together over it, like shaking sand off at the beach. Ralston looked over his shoulder simultaneously to be sure he wasn't susceptible to a sneak attack from behind, when suddenly his crumb clapping resulted in his tipping the can over.

The metal can fell over like a two-ton bell, clanging against the floor as trash fell out.

Before Sister Ann Bernadette could unfold herself from her indignant stance, and run over and clamp a body scissors on Ralston, he managed to manually sweep the spilled junk back into the can and skip off to his seat.

Ralston missed lunch that day, and the class paid for his stupidity, too. Ralston's stunt was the kind of foolishness that the nuns dedicated their lives to stopping. They took vows to prevent kids from this sort of tomfoolery. They swore on a stack of Bibles and in the name of Jesus Christ that no kid will ever get away with any form of goofiness without a full-fledged retaliatory response.

That day, thanks to Ralston, Sister Ann Bernadette B-52'd us with homework. She dropped assignments on us in Religion, English, Math, Geography; even gave us Art homework. At the end of the day, kids were going home carrying five textbooks, their three-ring notebook, and their reading workbook.

As we lined up that day in the classroom to leave, each kid stood like Quasimodo, hunched over with an armful of books on his or her hip. These were the days before book bags. Any mis-balancing of the books under one's arm could send an avalanche of hard covers tumbling to the floor.

All kids at I.C. knew the feeling of having their books go flying from beneath their arm. You just hoped it didn't happen while you were climbing onto the bus or walking down the staircase. For some reason, it's one of life's most embarrassing moments, picking up a pile of your books after you've had them jump from your grasp. Other people around you seem to take particular delight out of your struggles to rebalance the load, too.

It was a popular bully tactic to knock the books out from someone's arms, but it wasn't done at I.C. In fact, I.C. never had student bullies. The nuns were the bullies. A kid bullying another kid simply was too redundant to make sense.

Why did she become a nun? Well, let's just say she wasn't exactly a paragon of pulchritudity.

SISTERHOOD: IT'S NO BEAUTY PAGEANT!

Immaculate Conception's nuns were regarded by us kids as the elite order of all sisterhood. Why? Because the nuns told us they were the best order of nuns, that's why. They called themselves the Sisters of Loretto. In nine years of schooling, we were never given any explanation as to who the Sisters of Loretto were, or why they were, or who supported them. Never heard a nun mention any other order of nuns, either.

We figured Loretto must be a foreign country somewhere hell bent on the domination of America's Catholic kids. There in the nation of Loretto, this band of renegades replenished their ranks, raising and training these deranged, social misfits to become shrouded Stormtroopers on behalf of Roman Catholicism.

They wore black habits. Walking black shrouds from head to toe. Large nuns and small nuns. Each looking like a moving black curtain. Black heeled shoes barely poked out from under their frock, enabling each nun's step to be disguised. A walking nun moved like she was on a moving sidewalk. Imperceptible steps.

They wore white cowls over their heads, like Batman, and a long, black veil that fell down their backs. Their head seemed to be framed by a white cardboard that clamped onto their veils somehow. I've seen nuns walk in 50 mile per hour winds and never lose that cardboard/veil get-up.

They also wore a white cardboard chest protector, like a catcher, its function I cannot even imagine. It was like a white, over-starched bib.

Down their right side was their rosary beads, featuring large, black stones and a heavy metal cross.

In nine years, I never saw a nun actually use these rosary beads. Never saw a nun pray with them. Never saw a nun tie up a kid with them, either. But they were never without their rosary beads. I guess a nun couldn't be a humble servant of God without her lariat of rosary beads.

Each nun looked like the other from a distance. Somehow, though, you could tell them apart instantly. There were no dainty nuns. No Bo Dereks in the crowd. Generally, a nun is not a paragon of pulchritude. In fact, most nuns had a face that would chase a dog up a tree. Large noses, big mouths, wire-rimmed glasses, crunched eyebrows. Pointed or flabby chins. Yellow teeth. No makeup, of course. They were beauties, all right.

You could imagine them getting dressed in the morning. Helping each other on with their gear, like Huns getting ready for battle every day. You couldn't help but think of them as Huns. Spinoffs of Attila. Huns...Nuns.. it all made sense.

Obviously, over the years, The Sisters of Loretto evolved from huns to nuns, and took on the look of ninjas. Every possible show of skin was covered, lest they look sexy, God forbid. No hair showing, ever. The cowl took care of that. They all could have been bald, for all I knew. It was deemed ungodly, I guess, to show hair. Certainly, Sister Alphonsa's mustache and Sister Mary Barbara's mole hairs were exemptions.

THE HOUSE UP ON THE HILL

ılate Conception, the nuns lived
: hill, in the Convent next to the
nd in back of the church.

ing, if you were at school early,
lozen nuns in double file drifting
lk toward the school. They didn't
er. At least they didn't turn their
ıer's direction. They marched du-
e school, together, but separately.
ıt that one nun was friends, par-
ıother. There was no sense that
y got along together or hated one
uld understand them hating each
other. Imagine having to live under the same roof
with twenty nuns, then having to teach in the
same facility all day, too.

The Convent was a spooky old building, four
stories high. It was made of white brick that had
yellowed over the past 45 years. There were little

windows all over the place, yet the windows didn't seem to let light in. You couldn't see through the windows or discern that there was any life inside. Each window was like a dark shadow, even when the sun was shining on the building. As kids, we imagined the nuns in there praying all the time. Chapels everywhere. Candlelight was the only means of illumination. Nobody I knew had ever been in the creepy, old house. We figured the place probably was a replica of the Tower of London: chains on the walls, perhaps a stock or two for detaining bad kids who were about to absorb a whipping. It wouldn't have surprised me to hear occasional cries of insanity coming from the building.

One year, Volare, Womsley and I decided we'd pay the Convent a visit during Halloween. It was the perfect time to get a peek inside of the old rat trap. Maybe catch a glimpse of the nuns running around in their skivvies. After all, they couldn't possibly be wearing that nun outfit day and night. I figured they each had lockers, and after school they yanked off the habit and cardboard and beads and jumped into the showers, like a football team does. Probably snap towels at each other's asses for fun, then slipped into pajamas the rest of the day.

Halloween was the perfect day for a visit to the Convent. The place was borderline haunted, anyhow. The ghouls that currently lived inside made the visit all the spookier. Best of all, we were disguised so well in our Halloween makeup, the nuns wouldn't even know it was us.

So, we stepped up on the concrete porch and rang the doorbell, which was an annoying buzzer. I guess after hearing school bells every day, and church bells and altar bells, they didn't want a door bell, per se. A buzzer was much better to a nun. Like the sound you'd hear right before the trap door released beneath you, sending you falling into a pit of hungry tigers.

A few moments later, there was the sound of someone coming to the door. It was a long walk to the door, apparently. And then, there were three doors to open before even seeing us. First a windowed door, then another metal door, then a screen door. These nuns must never leave the house, I figured. Who'd want to open so many doors just to get the hell out of there?

To our surprise, an elderly woman that we'd never seen before, wearing street clothes, welcomed us on the porch. Who in the Christ is this, we thought. Could this be one of the nuns incognito?

We bellowed out "Trick or treat" and waited to see how this nun impostor would react. She smiled at us, perhaps chuckling at our pathetic impersonations of G.I. soldiers. Volare was dressed as our Viet Cong prisoner. We carried our rifles in one hand and our bag of candy in the other.

"Oh, my goodness. Come inside, boys. Come on...I've got some cookies for you."

She shooed us into the house like letting in a fly, apparently didn't want to let the stale air escape from the convent. She led us down a creaky, wood-floored hallway toward the kitchen. To the right, we could see a dimly lit living room with a black and white TV on, but nobody in the room watching it. I saw an open TV Guide on the old, brown Salvation Army-style couch, but no other signs of normal living. I was surprised at the sight of the TV Guide, realizing it wasn't a prayer book or Bible.

Whatever did the nuns watch on television? Can't watch Bishop Sheen all day long. Do they watch Bewitched? Get Smart? Let's Make a Deal? I'd bet my bottom dollar they watch The Twilight Zone and the Three Stooges. I'm certain that many nuns studied Moe Howard's array of pugilistic techniques. Or maybe they taught him a thing or two.

Surely they watch The Flying Nun and criticize it without mercy. I could imagine them mocking Sister Bertrille, aka Sally Field, wearing all white instead of black, and showing head hair and looking all pixie and cute. And the gall to be friendly and happy, and soar like a bird all over the county, for Christ aloud. The nuns must have despised that show. Hell, I hated it myself. What producers in their right minds would make a hero out of a nun? In real life, a nun like Sister Bertrille would make for good skeet shooting.

I noticed in the corner under a crucifix was a hi-fidelity record player and radio. The lid was open showing the turntable, but I noticed there were no records around.

What did the nuns listen to? The Beatles? Yeah, right. The Stones? Ha! Maybe they twisted to Chubby Checker on the weekends. Perhaps the nuns jived to some cool jazz, or jitterbugged with each other, like convicts, to Elvis' Jailhouse Rock.

Nah. I was sure they listened to the Singing Nun strumming her guitar to "Dominique." Or when they were really in the mood for rocking, they spun a few Mormon Tabernacle Choir albums.

We proceeded in tow behind this friendly old woman who led us into this antiquated, dim-lighted kitchen. It became apparent to me that the nuns must have eyes like owls, able to see in the dark at all hours of the day. My eyes already were burning from the dimness.

"Help yourselves, boys," the nice woman said, pointing to the cookie plate piled high with oatmeal cookies. "Would you like some milk, boys?"

Suddenly, it dawned on us collectively that we were loitering around in the Convent. Christ Almighty, it's Halloween, it's after school, and we're hanging around inside the Convent about to have milk and cookies. If we don't get out of here right now, I thought, we could get trapped having a religious lesson or asked to read a passage out of the Bible, for shit sakes. Or have the meaning of Halloween—a hallowed eve—explained to us for the thousandth time.

"No, we better be going, thanks anyway," I said as I pulled Womsley's hands off an Oatmeal cookie, making him drop it back onto the plate. We don't want to be obligated over a goddam oatmeal cookie, I figured.

As I turned to vamoose, I caught movement of someone watching us from up on the staircase. It was a woman, and it wasn't a black shrouded nun. She ducked behind the wall, but not before I caught a glimpse. It wasn't anyone I recognized, but then who would I recognize that wasn't in full nun garb? I wondered if the whole gang of nuns was out in the streets trick-or-treating, dressed in jeans, T-shirts and tennis shoes.

Then we heard the ceiling creaking above us, as a herd of nuns must have been stirring around. That's when Volare and Womsley picked up the pace and beat me to the front door.

"Bye. Bye," we said to the nice, old woman who we later surmised was the nuns' cook. We sped down the creaking hallway and crammed ourselves through the three-door exit, each guy having his chance at being first. We each leaped from the four-step porch and dashed from the building, looking like costumed burglars carrying our treat bags full of loot.

It was a narrow escape. A true adventure. Yet somehow the story we later told to our friends didn't translate into anything mysterious or thrilling.

Our friends wouldn't have been impressed unless we said Sister Mary Barbara came tumbling down the staircase in a wheelchair like Norman Bates' mother in Psycho.

GREETINGS

They called each other by their formal names.

"Thank you, Sister Ann Bernadette."

"Sister Eileen, would you mind turning my classroom lights off after class?"

You'd think they'd have pet names for each other, like we had for them. You know, like, "Hey, Shortie, how 'bout flippin' the lights for me later, huh?" Or, "Morning, Goober. How's it hangin'?"

The nuns stuck to the book at all times. No levity outside the classroom. Inside the classroom there was humor allowed, but it had to be satire or sarcasm based on some sort of humiliation of a student.

Like the time Ron Tazmilio got suckered into Sister Veronica's trap. The crafty penguin asked individual kids for plurals of words:

Marsha: boat. "Boats," she replied.

Sarah: house. "Houses," she responded.

Kevin: school. "Schools," he said.

Ronald: child. "Childs," proclaimed Tazmilio. The nun rushed up infront of his face and said mockingly, "Oh, yes, Ronald, look at all the childs!"

The class broke up in hysterical laughter at Tazmilio's silly gaffe, each student secretly grateful for not being chosen, for every one of us would have been tricked into saying "childs" just as Tazmilio had.

But that's how the nuns got their jollies. Somewhere along the line, Tazmilio must have pissed off Sister Veronica, and she nailed him at a time of her choosing.

While nuns chose their moments to punish kids—even if they had to lay a trap to get them— they also tended to reward certain sycophantic kids who had a penchant for sucking ass. Those obsequious little bastards could usually be found sitting in the first aisle and the first seat. Here, one's responsibility was to answer the door when somebody knocked. It was a real honor to get up out of your seat when all others were relegated to their chairs for the past four hours. But to answer the door as if the classroom were your own house, well, that was Congressional Medal of Honor stuff.

There were other dubious honors awarded to kids by the nuns, like erasing the blackboard, clapping the erasers together after school, passing out mimeographed papers, or collecting assigned work from students, desk to desk.

All those honors were secondary compared to the privilege bestowed onto the kid who answered the door.

One of the rules of I.C. was that each class had to stand and bark out a greeting, in unison, to every person who visited the classroom. This became an annoyance that students grew to endure.

If Sister Ann Dominic paid a visit to our classroom, upon her entering the room, the entire class would have to rise and say, in harmony, "Good morning Sister Ann Dominic, how are you?"

The visitor would respond as they saw fit. Sometimes the nun would answer, "I'm fine, class, thank you," then get on with her business. Other times, the visitor would simply ignore the 30 kids chiming out the greeting. Still others would say things like, "Oh, aren't we in good spirits today!"

The trick to greeting visitors in unison was to know when to start. Usually, one of the smart kids would begin the greeting with an exaggeratedly drawn out—"Gooooooood mmmmorrrrnnning..." allowing the rest of the class to get their timing with the remainder of the greeting.

It became funny when the same visitor would duck back into the class for a repeat conversation five minutes later only to have the class rise and start the perfunctory locution all over again. This always ticked off both the host nun and the visitor. The nun would gruffly tell the class to sit back down. We knew we were being stupid, greeting the same person five minutes apart, but it was sort of a rebellion. The nuns taught us to greet each visitor to the classroom in this vocal manner. So we did. They never mentioned what to do if the same person goes in and out of the classroom. We figured, if you don't like the sing-song greeting of 30 disingenuous kids, then stay the hell out!

UNIFORMS
OF THE
INDENTURED

The first time you walked into a classroom at I.C., you noticed immediately that every boy was dressed the same. Every girl, too. Having kids wear uniforms was the perfect solution for demanding uniformity.

Clothing in today's society becomes a personal statement or expression. In the public schools, kids wore anything they wanted, just about: slacks or jeans, dresses, pants, or shorts. They grew their hair long, and combed it whatever way they chose. Or maybe they didn't comb it at all. Personality was expressed by the way a kid presented him or herself at school.

At Immaculate Conception, a kid wore the same thing every day. The same as the kid next to him. He expressed no personality, and there was no individualism. And that was fine with the nuns. They didn't express any individuality themselves.

Every school day of my childhood life I wore a tan button-down shirt and a brown necktie that conveniently hooked around the neck. By trial and error, the tie could be adjusted around the neck by messing with the metal clamp that determined the length. This became an important skill in a boy's life, knowing how to quickly adjust the length of the tie clasp under the collar, to stave off strangulation.

If someone were to tug violently on your tie while it was around your neck—which, by the way, was more of a common occurrence than you might think—you could unclamp the tie from under your collar before your carotid artery pinched off the blood to your brain. Emergency tie-undoing was an important technique of survival at Catholic School, since a boy's tie precariously dangled just below his chin straight down to his waist, serving as a handy leash for nuns.

To a nun, the tie must have seemed like bait; like a fisherman's alluring jig is to a wall-eyed trout. Dangling and teasing just below his chin, few nuns could resist an occasional yank, or pull, or tug or twist. It was the adjustable tie that enabled a nun to swing a kid around into any desired position.

Out of line. Into line. Over here. Up front here. Come here. Pay attention...

Like a rope, though, the tie was only good for pulling. Even a nun couldn't push a kid around by his tie. So the nuns just pushed you by the chest. She could stop your momentum backward at any time by quickly grabbing your tie, thus straightening you back up.

After nine years of wearing tan shirts and a brown tie along with brown shoes and socks, I've never worn brown clothing again. I actually O.D.'d on brown for a lifetime. I haven't owned a pair of brown socks since 8th grade. Or brown shoes. And why would anyone ever wear a brown tie?

The girls had to wear what has come to be known as Catholic plaid. They wore white blouses and vests, every school day. The girls hated the uniforms, especially when school was out and they were walking around town. It was like having a big "P" on you, or like walking around in prison stripes. There was no prestige in being seen in your school uniform. The obligatory apparel was simply a reminder to all that you were a conscript of Immaculate Conception.

Interestingly, whenever it was picture-taking day at I.C., the order to students was to wear regular clothing. Boys were encouraged to wear a sports jacket, or at least a dress shirt and tie. Girls had to wear a white blouse, but didn't have to wear the plaid for that day only.

I don't understand why it was allowed to show for posterity the kids in regular clothing, when every other day they were confined to uniforms. As one looks back on those I.C. days through school photos, there is no sign of uniforms. Except for Tazmilio, the kid who forgets it's picture day and shows up in his school uniform anyhow. His photo is the only record of the real truth of uniforms.

Uniforms were a break for parents. They never worried about what their kids where wearing to school the next day. There was no problem when it came to "Back to School" shopping days in late August, when other parents are dragging their kids along on expensive, clothes-shopping sprees.

All parents had to do was buy the plaid ensembles for the girls or the tan shirts and brown ties for the boys from the school. I'm sure I.C. made a pretty penny on the uniform sales, too. My parents were angry way out of proportion when I came home with a ruined tie or a torn shirt. They acted as if the cost of replacing a shirt would bankrupt the family, sending us to the proverbial poor farm, where we'd now be forced to eat alfalfa and soybean out of horse troughs.

SCALPED TO THE BONE

The one great advantage to wearing uniforms was getting dressed in the morning. It took about 19 seconds for me to get dressed. Speed dressing was a necessity since I always avoided getting up until the last possible second.

Getting up early for school only prolonged the day. I preferred to make it a race against the bus. Every morning was havoc, pushing the envelope of procrastination.

When the alarm went off, I rolled out of bed, and splashed some water on my face and brushed my teeth at the same time. Then I toweled off and jumped into a pair of pants and shirt while slipping on socks and shoes. Every morning it was a slightly different order. Socks always before shoes, of course. But sometimes the shirt went on before the pants. Sometimes not. Sometimes the belt remained in the loops from the day before. Sometimes not. Usually I stuck my tie in my pocket and put it on while on the bus.

It was senseless to worry about combing my hair. Like all boys at I.C., there wasn't much hair to mess with. Most kids like me were buzz cut.

My father sent me to the worst barber in town—Hector the Barber—who everybody knew was nuts. Everyone else went to Bob and Tom's Barber Shop, where you were assured of not getting totally scalped.

Not at Hector's. The old man was a bit senile, and he'd cut my hair while jabbering on about the same old uninteresting story of how he cut the head off a chicken and it ran around the barn for an hour, headless. I heard him tell this moronic story dozens of times, each time while he proceeded to scalp me like a Mohican.

My parents instructed me to ask for a "Princeton" haircut, obviously because they thought it made me seem smart. To Hector, a "Princeton" haircut was the same as a "Parris Island" hairdo. Cut and cut until the scissors were rendered useless.

Hector invariably sent me out of his shop with nary a hair left to blow in the breeze. In the wintertime, my fresh hair scalping was so short, my stocking cap didn't fit for a month. I could practically spin my stocking cap around my head.

It was difficult keeping the Chicago Bears logo at the front of the cap after one of Hector's defoliations.

There was nothing like the chilly feeling brought on by the Chicago winter, while stepping outside Hector's barber shop after a shearing. The wind would knife right through my stocking cap and penetrate the suddenly hairless bone between my ears. Instantly, the winters became colder after Hector was through converting me into a Hari-Kristina look-a-like.

Every morning, it was a sprint to the bus stop. It was also a coordination test getting out of the house in the morning. I grabbed my three-ring notebook and my textbooks and notebooks, stacked them according to size, and corralled them under my left arm. Then, I'd grab a donut from the breakfast table and jam it halfway in my mouth while reaching for my brown-bag lunch. Then I'd flip the light switch off with my nose and grab for the door and close it while descending the stairs.

I'd take off in a trot for the bus stop, three blocks away, while chewing the donut. I constantly adjusted the books under my arm to avoid an avalanche, and hooked my lunch bag in my baby finger of my left hand, and used the now-free right arm for balance and swinging momentum. Once I got up over the slight hill of Burton Avenue, I could tell if the Immaculate Conception bus was in view. Often times, the top of the big yellow bus would show over the horizon, sending me into a full gallop toward the bus stop.

It was taboo to make Armando the bus driver wait for you. It was a tacit understanding. Each I.C. kid was expected to be at the bus stop and board the bus in single file and quietly. I was the exception. More times than not, I was in full sprint toward the bus, reaching the collapsing doors just as the last kid at the bus stop reached the top step.

I saw this photo finish arrival at the bus stop as perfect bus-catching management. Spent like a marathon runner at the finish line, I'd grunt out a "Good morning, Armando!" while gasping for breath. Armando never answered. I'm not exactly sure whether he even spoke English or not. Maybe he eked out a "Morning" when he was especially inspired in the morning. But even a foreigner can do that proficiently. I know he wasn't a mute, but he sure was a taciturn sort.

It was a successful morning when I finally collapsed into a seat like a ton of bricks knowing that I had achieved bus management perfection.

Some days, Armando was late due to the weather or the mere circumstances of having to make three routes to school, picking up and dropping off three loads of kids with the same bus.

Seldom did I have time or the desire to socialize with the kids of varying ages at the bus stop. Mostly, kids stood quietly, almost mournfully, kicking a stone around, or idly milling around in a circle like prisoners in a prison yard, ruefully anticipating the day ahead.

Every kid stood at the bus stop hoping beyond hope that maybe this day, this fortunate day of days, the bus wouldn't come. If only Armando would quit, or the school just not notice that the "Third Mary"—that was the last round of the second of two buses—had skipped a route.

Whenever I was at the bus stop waiting, I always wished the bus wouldn't come. Unless it was below freezing. Then I wished it to be there immediately.

But usually, the sight of that big, yellow monstrosity coming up Burton Avenue with its top lights flashing was a dream buster. It was always a relief making the bus, which I missed just once in my entire school career. Through rain, sleet and snow, Armando was always there. Never early, but occasionally late. It didn't matter. Since my neighborhood was always relegated to the final bus of the day, we were expected to be late once in a while.

I preferred sitting in the back of the bus. The older I got, the more assured I was of sitting wherever I wanted. Kids just seem to sense whose seat is whose. Ideally, the back seat by the window allowed you to put your head on the glass and bump along with the bus's rattling and bouncing. With my skull resting on the window, my brain would rattle 100 times a minute as the bus vibrated its way to school. Somehow this was soothing, have a mental milkshake before school.

I found out years later that some schoolgirls enjoyed sitting in the seats just above the tires, where the excessive bounce and vibration became a sort of physical therapy comparable to that of a coin-operated mattress in a cheap hotel.

When Armando got up a head of steam on Green Bay Road, the back of the bus resembled a roller coaster. There were a few dips in the road that sent the kids airborne for a split second, like turbulence in an aircraft.

When we'd approach the railroad tracks, however, the rush down Green Bay Road became a moot point. Armando was instructed by Immaculate Conception's principal to wait at the tracks if he could see even the slightest sign of a train in the distance.

Sometimes we'd sit at the tracks for 10 minutes waiting for a light down the tracks about as visible as the North Star to arrive. The north suburbs of Chicago had made news almost yearly for car-pooling housewives getting plowed over by onrushing commuter trains.

The Northwestern line headed to The Loop in Chicago carrying briefcase wielding suits in the morning, and dragged them back to their hometown in suburbia in the evening. Every road had crossings that always worked, but still people managed to get steamrolled by trains at the crossings. So, our bus driver waited patiently for this train to arrive and pass every morning. The nuns made sure we didn't get killed on the railroad tracks. It was much more preferred, I guess, to siphon the life out of us right there at school, day in and day out.

Armando was usually our bus driver. But every other year or so, the brain trust of Immaculate Conception would alter the bus route. The first day of school we might find that old Joe McCrarren, who drove the other bus, "The Loretto," was picking us up.

Old Joe was a curmudgeon who looked like W.C. Fields after a few martinis. Joe never talked to the kids, either, except for a rare, "Sit down and shut up!" warning when things got out of hand on the school-bound conveyance.

I liked Joe despite his gruff demeanor. Once in a while when I said hello or goodbye on the bus, he'd grunt acknowledgingly. Most kids, however, were afraid to communicate with old Joe. They usually looked at him cautiously when boarding the bus, and swung themselves down the stairs quickly when leaving.

The life of a bus driver at I.C. was a thankless one. We never saw these guys cleaning the bus or warming up the engine in the freezing, early mornings. All we knew was, they were never absent. Always on the job. And during the day, they did routine maintenance of the school.

Every teacher knew that my arrival to the classroom meant the final bus had arrived, and class could begin. I was never in my seat longer than two seconds before class began. I was the personification of the day's beginning. I don't know how long the teacher waited to start class until realizing I was going to be absent on that particular day. Probably waited until lunchtime before giving up on my attendance.

This was the typical I.C. classroom. Years later, the lift-top desks were gone, replaced by the adult-sized, lefty-hating desk-chair.

THE JANITOR: LIFE AT THE BOTTOM

Mr. Ciancetti, the school's janitor, was an immigrant sycophant who saw the nuns as saints. He had been the janitor at I.C. for as long as the school had been there—since 1946 or so—yet he still had his thick, Italian accent.

Mr. Ciancetti didn't have a first name as far as anybody knew. It was probably something like Luigi or Rodolfo, some name that would make you want to call him Mr. Ciancetti.

Well, the nuns loved him because Mr. Ciancetti would do virtually anything for them, like a penitent sinner trying to gain brownie points to heaven. As if being kind to a nun was a way to champion a spiritual run to heaven. Mr. Ciancetti would make me sick with his obsequious beckoning of the nuns when entering their classrooms.

"Mornin' shishter," he'd sing in his thick, Sicilian accent.

"Oh, Mr. Ciancetti, I'm glad you're here," a nun would say. "Would you mind cleaning up the horseshit in the back of the room, please? The children and I had a horseshit fight, and we all had lots of fun slinging the dung all over the room. But now we're done, so could you clean it up, please?"

A request like this would send Mr. Ciancetti into a thousand thank yous, like a bowing Chinese peasant grateful to be in the presence of such a holy, Catholic icon as a nun.

Mr. Ciancetti's job was probably the worst one in America, too, as far as us kids could tell. It was Mr. Ciancetti who got the call when a pupil lost his cookies in the classroom. Puking kids at I.C. was quite a common occurrence, especially in the lower grades.

It wasn't that the food was bad in the cafeteria. It was the fact that the nuns and certain lay teachers scared the hell out of kids; enough to make their stomachs a curdling volcano.

Old lady Sezzo's classroom was Mr. Ciancetti's hell on earth. He got the call to spread sawdust over Sezzo's floor about once a week. The old janitor would show up wheeling a cart with a metal trash can, a shovel, a broom, and a 50-pound can of sawdust.

Every nun either was a contending pugilist or wanted to be one, it seemed. If you dropped your guard as a pupil, there was always the threat of a nun sucker punching

you to get your attention. If you knew what was good for you, you kept your head on a swivel. Nuns were known for their "mistaken identity" blows, especially if you looked like you were chewing gum. If you happened to be in a mood for a beating, all you had to do was move your jaw up and down about three times.

SEZZO, THE RUTHLESS TYRANT

Sezzo's eight-year-olds were puking and pissing all over the place. The old lady just freaked kids out, including me. For some idiotic reason, the Immaculate Conception geniuses thought the Gestapo-style teaching of the 64 year-old Martina Sezzo was ideal for eight year olds.

This vicious, gray and steelwool-haired tyrant was the cruelest person I ever met. She took her life's frustrations out on the third graders just as most nuns relieved their anxieties at the kids' expense. Sezzo was a religious woman, too, who saw her torturing third graders as her call of duty.

About 5 foot tall, old lady Sezzo had wire rimmed glasses, pouchy cheeks, a big, thick body, and a slaphappy nature about her. Not that she was happy, just slappy. She slapped kids first, and asked questions later, if at all. Unbelievable that she saw third graders as the age necessary for intimidation, sarcasm, humiliation and physical punishment. Sezzo was a nun in sheep's clothing to me. Even worse.

My year in third grade was the longest, most regrettable year of my life. And for one reason only: Mrs. Sezzo. If I had a chance to come back to earth after death and relive my experiences, I'd have to negotiate a change to third grade. I wouldn't relive that eternal year again if it meant being king.

Sezzo was always afraid that kids were pulling the wool over her eyes. Even third graders. She wasn't going to tolerate talking or fooling around on her watch. No matter what. In her former life she may have been Genghis Khan.

Sezzo was most suspicious of kids wanting to go to the bathroom. She was convinced that an eight-year-old's bladder had no excuse to be overflowing during class time. So, she decreed that there would be no excuses for bathroom privileges while class was under way. We broke for breaks at designated times only. And they were few and far between.

In these days before air conditioning, there was no compensation for cold or drafty days, or the potential consequences on a child's bladder.

Raising your hand to obtain Sezzo's permission to go to the bathroom took the courage of a war hero, or the utter desperation of a dying kid. It was usually the latter.

Many times I found myself mired in a death-defying struggle to keep from peeing all over the room. The mere idea that Sezzo discouraged kids from leaving the classroom to go to the bathroom was enough psychologically to make a kid have to go, sometimes.

If you got desperate enough, you might choose to raise your hand and ask to go to the bathroom. Sezzo typically would ignore the kid's raised hand for a while until the kid finally dropped his hand in despair.

Occasionally, Sezzo would answer with a stern, "What is it, big boy?"

Many times, Sezzo would answer the request for a trip to the bathroom with an admonishment to the class, creating embarrassment for the kid while sending a message of potential humiliation to the next person who requests such an ill-timed privilege.

Sezzo was convinced that kids were so devil-ish- minded that they would feign having to go to the bathroom only to trot off to the john to lol-lygag around, and thereby show her up. Never did she consider giving a kid the benefit of the doubt.

Sezzo's logic was simply stated to a belea-guered kid. "If I let you go, then I'll have to let the whole class go...and we'll never get any work done, will we, big girl! Now put your hand down and do your work."

When Sezzo would refuse a kid a trip to the bathroom, panic would set in in the kid's face. I know, it happened to me a half-dozen or more times. Every kid in the class knew what it was like to be forced to hold his kidneys back.

It was impossible to concentrate if you were the victim of this urinary urge. The rest of the class now was concentrating on your body language, try-ing to assess the degree of your desperation. It was easy to tell where on the urinary Richter scale a kid was at. Both girls and boys crossed their legs first. I used to try and cross my legs twice, turning my legs into rope-like appendages, thus squeezing off any possible passage of pee that may be on the move.

When you're in third grade in Sezzo's class, you're going to experience pee depravation. The symptoms are classic. Once the urge strikes you, it's not long before the sweats come. Your forehead soon heats up, and you begin sweating under your collar and clip-on tie. Then your sweat turns cold, and you shiver for a while. When things get close to desperate, your eyes will fill up with tears, only you imagine it to be pee rising over your head. When desperation persists, you swivel your head around uncontrollably. You look around the room, trying to think of something else, but it is impossible.

I remember watching kids who had attempted to request a trip to the bathroom and were refused. They suffered the same way I did. I learned never to ask Sezzo for a bathroom trip, since I didn't want to tip off the whole class that I was desperate. All eyes would be on you, then, and that scrutiny only made it tougher.

If you had to go, you stared at the clock like Svengoli, trying to move the hands of the clock along by your will alone. But despite all the magical wizardry, it only made the clock move slower. All you could really do was pray. And hope that you didn't explode right there at your desk.

All this torture, it was never lost on me, was happening to a third grader. A kid no more than four feet high.

When the class finally ended, and we began to recess or have a bathroom trip, it was the scariest time of all. It always seemed to take the class five minutes to get up out of their chairs and out of the classroom. Now, moving around, it seemed to loosen the bladder and get it pumping again. That's when you were most threatened with peeing in your pants.

Many kids in Sezzo's class were forced to pee in their pants. The only thing is, peeing in one's pants is not where it ends. It's peeing all over the floor that is so humiliating. A urinary accident becomes an ignominious label on a kid that lasts a lifetime. The scuttlebutt that you had pissed on the floor would be all around the school like a thunder clap. Next thing you knew, all your friends and enemies in other classes would know. You'd be the laughing stock for weeks and months to come. If a girl pissed in her pants, she could expect to be a spinster the rest of her life, the humiliation would be so bad. A peeing boy would simply suffer the indignation as a diapered baby for the next fifty years.

It wasn't a pretty site when Silvia Fiore peed all over the floor one day in Sezzo's class. Suddenly, without warning during arithmetic class, Karen Williams blurts out, "Mrs.Sezzo, Silvia peed on the floor!"

Sezzo came waddling down Silvia's aisle to inspect the damage while the entire class stood along their desks for a view of the leak. Sezzo started grumbling disgustedly and sent Silvia out of the room, an idea that came about a minute too late, judging by the quart of pee on the floor. Sezzo dispatched Don Mintori to find Mr. Ciancetti and have him bring his sawdust accoutrement.

The next 15 minutes was spent watching the elderly Italian janitor perform a task that none of us could have done in our bravest moment. He moved desks out of the way, shoveled sawdust on the floor where Silvia peed, then shoveled and swept it up for disposal. To third graders, it was the grossest job in the world. But someone had to do it. We only wondered why it didn't have to be Sezzo.

While every kid felt sorry for Silvia and her excruciating embarrassment, we could never look at her again without thinking about her peeing on the floor. It was a label that would be permanent. So would the shame that befell Maria Erickson for the same incontinence. And Roy Sanchez. And Janice Jarrod.

Robert Corbett once pissed in his pants and proceeded through the day undaunted. The entire front of his brown corduroy pants were soaked in a wide circle, and he audibly squished and squashed when he walked. Yet he was unfazed by the ignominy of it all. He didn't act affected by the mishap throughout the day. Corbett deflected classmates' barbs and taunts like lint off his sleeve. Since it didn't seem to embarrass him, nobody thought much of it after a while.

Corbett proved that embarrassment is only brought on by oneself. However, there wasn't a kid in the class who wouldn't say he was an idiot. Maybe he wasn't humiliated by it, but he certainly proved to be a dork.

Corbett also proved that the hand dryers in the bathroom could be reasonably effective in evaporating pee dampness from one's pants over the course of the day.

There was only one thing more humiliating than peeing on the floor in Sezzo's class. That was blowing jowls all over yourself, as I managed to do in Sezzo's class.

One morning, I showed up in class with a bit of a stomach rumbling. It was about 10:15 a.m., and we had just opened up our readers for some classroom oral reading.

Suddenly, without much warning, I began to feel sick. I dared not draw any attention to myself lest have Sezzo descend on me for conspiring to ruin her precious classroom lesson.

It didn't take long, though, for my stomach to make a scene. Without recourse, I promptly puked all over my desk, right on top of my open reader. The distinctive noise of a stomach retching was unmistakable even to the kids sitting farthest away, in the front of the class.

Friends of mine forty years later can still remember old lady Sezzo trotting down the aisle, grabbing a towel out of thin air, and wrapping it around my head, nearly suffocating me. She led me out of the room by the towel like I was emitting toxic fumes or something, and more less tossed me toward the bathroom. Apparently, Sezzo was less enamored with kid puke than she was with kid pee.

The old bitty had no trouble sending me to the nurse and excusing me from class for the rest of the day. She didn't care to see any encore of my morning performance.

I was horrified by the accident, and dreaded my return to the classroom, even four days later. Unbelievably, Sezzo had Mr. Ciancetti salvage my reader despite the pages of chapter four being permanently bound together like a prison-circulated Playboy.

At I.C., kids rented the books from the school, which re-rented them over and over to incoming kids. It was forbidden for a student to write in his textbook. No doodling or underlining, either. Somebody the next year was treated to a rented reader with chapter four hermetically sealed by my stomach's regurgitation.

I wasn't around to see Mr. Ciancetti coagulate my cookies with his sawdust routine. But I saw him do it plenty of times in Sezzo's class. We figured that per year, Mr. Ciancetti shoveled the sawdust equivalent to that of an entire redwood.

Kids who forgot their homework at home in, say, Spelling, would get sick to their stomach and hork up their breakfasts at the thought of Sezzo's imminent scolding. Just the sight of that wicked, little battle axe coming down your aisle was enough to send stomach acids up your throat.

A thousand times, I remember Sezzo writing on the board with her flopping underarms swinging like voluptuous, nipple-less breasts with every syllable she wrote. She would turn suddenly to catch a kid talking, and head toward the kid in her classic, Captain Blythe limp. Five kids held their breath as Sezzo clogged down the aisle until she reached her target. Boy or girl, it didn't matter. Sezzo came up slapping or pulling. I don't remember the girls getting slapped, but they sure had their hair pulled and their cheeks grabbed. Boys were pummeled. On the back, lots of times. With books. But mostly sucker slapped with an open palm.

"What's the matter, big boy?" she always taunted. "Are you talking? Hmm? You wanna talk to me? Well, speak up, big boy!"

After absorbing a smacking, and with your head down on your desk in defeat, all you could see was her thick calves and ankles heading back up to the blackboard. She was the only woman I ever saw wear seamed hosiery. Her stocking toes stuck out of her open-toe shoes. Her big, thick heels clunk on the floor whenever she walked, like a pirate's wooden leg.

Her ratty, curly hair surely was impenetrable by any comb. She wore pearls every day. And her bifocal glasses had a clip-on chain holding them around her neck. Sezzo wanted to be a nun, you could tell. She was married, but had no kids (thank God).

Sezzo spoke of her beloved husband Bartholomew all the time. I used to pity the poor slob for having to come home to that wench every single day of his forlorn life. The only thing that kept me going as a third grader was knowing that some day, if Sezzo didn't kill me, I'd be heading into the fourth grade, thus leaving her in the dust of my most horrid memories.

Sezzo intimidated kids so badly that they'd do anything to avoid her wrath. Kids would rat on each other, even their best friends, for a moment of positive recognition from the old lady.

One day, I'm in the bathroom during a break from Sezzo's class, telling Dan Volare how much I hate Mrs. Sezzo. Another classmate, Joe Venici, hears my complaints, and tells me he's going to tell Mrs. Sezzo what I said. I laughed at him, thinking he was out of his mind for even considering such a betrayal. Nevertheless, Venici, before my unbelieving eyes, walked up to Mrs. Sezzo and proclaimed loud enough for the class to hear.

"Mrs. Sezzo..." Venici said.

"What is it?" grumbled the grouch.

"Um, I heard Richard in the bathroom say that, um, that he hated you."

I was astonished. And dumbfounded. I started denying the accusation like a bastard, whining and crying and carrying on like a true liar.

Sezzo certainly knew by my carrying on that it was true. The rest of the class knew it was true, too, since who DIDN'T hate Mrs. Sezzo?

Sezzo didn't have the decency or the common sense to diffuse the whole thing. Instead, she says to me, "Well, Mister, you don't have to like me, and I don't have to like you!"

I groveled my denials through tears all the way to my seat, wondering who I hated more, Sezzo or Venici.

BATHROOM BUFFOONERY

For some reason, I never bludgeoned Venici over the head with a pick ax for that episode. I think I may have figured that he was getting back at me for the humiliation I and a bunch of classmates used to cause him in the bathroom. Venici always was prone to having to take a dump during school. He had some kind of bowel problem. So, whenever he was in the stall, we would literally annoy the crap out of him. We'd do hand puppets under the stall, or chin ourselves over the stall for a peak down below. Or we'd rattle the door and tell him there was a fire drill in progress. Sometimes we'd grab his shoe from under the stall and threaten to drag him right off the bowl. Landry could do a funny imitation of Sister Mary Olive barging into the bathroom, calling out Venici's name.

Venici often got even with us for our hooligan behavior. He was never generous with the courtesy flush, and often times had us scurrying out of the john gasping for fresh air.

Nobody, and I mean nobody, risked taking a dump at school unless there was no alternative short of crapping in your pants. And even then, you tried to wait until recess so you could find a vacant john somewhere. Crapping in a crowded bathroom was something I never even attempted at I.C.

The bathroom was the setting for a bit of buffoonery at I.C. Since a kid was under so much scrutiny the whole day long, the bathroom was just about the only place a kid could be without a nun or other teacher breathing down his or her neck.

The girls used to get yelled at a lot by the nuns and teachers in the bathroom. But they couldn't do a whole lot of nonsense in the bathroom without the teacher storming in on them.

Immaculate Conception had no male teachers. And most nuns wouldn't barge into the boys' room. If they heard talking or fooling around, they'd fling the big door open and holler inside. Sometimes a nun would open the door and bend down to the floor to look under the stalls. The urinals in the boys' room were behind the stalls, so a nun could only hope to recognize the kids' shoes.

I.C. boys were smart to the nuns peering under the stalls, and often hung onto the urinals with their feet on the lip of the porcelain, thus exposing no feet on the floor.

I was in the bathroom when Sister Agnes Marita barged into the john and caught Kevin O'Brien with his feet off the ground, hanging on to the urinal. The slapping that ensued was hysterical, I must admit. She chased him out of the bathroom, slapping the back of his head while he attempted to pull up his zipper and duck her onslaught.

One time, one of the eighth graders adroitly dragged the large, brown, metal trash can behind the push-in door as he left the bathroom, setting up the next unsuspecting person who entered the bathroom with a noisy collision.

That random victim turned out to be John Sarducci. He was a fat, smart kid who never did anything wrong, and had a heart of gold. Yet his number of fate was called, and he paid the price. That's the way it was at I.C. Even the innocent go to the whipping post now and then.

Sarducci flung open the bathroom door, thus sending the big tubular can flying and tumbling like a Bouncing Betsy across the floor. By the time the large can was done careening off the floor and walls, Sister Mary Olive was out of her neighboring classroom looking for blood.

When the nun found Sarducci alone trying to erect the can with a horrified look on his face, the nun let fly with a two-fisted assault.

"Where do you think you are, young man, in the playground?" she screamed. She belted Sarducci as he tried to mumble out a plausible excuse.

"But, but, but...I, I, I...when the door...I didn't..." he stuttered, stunned by the sudden turn of events of going to take a piss one minute to being belted by a nun from another grade, the next minute.

Sarducci was reported to his teacher, Sister Veronica, for disturbing the seventh grade class by making unprecedented racket in the bathroom. After all the hullabaloo that ensued, it was understandable why Sarducci didn't have to take a piss after all. I noticed one thing that changed about Sarducci after that day: he always opened the bathroom door very slowly the rest of his I.C. days, lest there be a garbage can lurking right behind the door waiting for a grand entrance.

The bathroom was that unique setting where guys got together, and, for even just a minute, could have some pretty unusual ideas.

Dan Volare had his life flash before his eyes after a stunt he decided to pull in the bathroom one afternoon in seventh grade.

It was a mild February day, and Volare noticed that a ledge full of snow had accumulated on the windowsill of the bathroom. He got the ingenious idea to reach through the window, grab a handful of snow, form a snowball, and let fly at the next unsuspecting sucker who walked through the door.

As Volare and I laughed about his upcoming stunt and as he prepared to pitch a high fastball at the noggin of the next entrant, the door swung open. Volare wound up like Juan Marichal and was about to fire a raising fastball at the victim, when he saw that the sucker at the door was Sister Daniel Marie.

My mouth and eyes opened with fear as I envisioned the snowball smacking the old sourpuss right between the eyes. Miraculously, Volare balked, sending the snowball dribbling out of his hand instead of at rocket force, as intended.

Sister Daniel Marie stared at Volare in contempt as his follow-through momentum sent him toward her. She reached inside the door and grabbed him by the tie and dragged him like a mule to the classroom. She made him stand in the corner for an hour for that stunt that went unexplained to the rest of the class.

Later, at recess, I was happy to recount the episode to the amusement of all.

The cafeteria hasn't changed except the clock is gone. The tables and benches fold up into the wall—quite an innovation for those days. They were able to jam the whole school into this room for lunch at certain time intervals.

LUNCH TIME

Everything was a big production at Immaculate Conception when it came to doing things as a group. The nuns tried to make every day activities almost military-like, with order, discipline and quiet as priorities.

At I.C., the bells only rang to start school and to end it. Every grade had its own time for lunch. There were two sections of the school; the older part was the main building that housed kindergarten through second grade. It was the older section that had the main facilities, such as the cafeteria, principal's office, nurse's office, bookstore, and gymnasium.

Each class had its own schedule for going to lunch. The younger the kids, the earlier they ate. The idea was to avoid big kids stomping all over the little ones at lunchtime. So, each class had to make its trek to the cafeteria, where tables and benches folded down from the wall to accommodate a couple hundred kids.

The nuns had an ingenious method for getting kids to eat quickly and leave the cafeteria, making room for other kids. They allowed only 30 minutes for lunch. That means, a kid who valued his recess, had to gobble his food down to salvage any decent time outside.

At I.C., even the paltry recess time was important to most kids. Being cooped up all day in the same desk in the same classroom looking at the same nun was enough to send anyone outside screaming like a raving Banshee.

When lunchtime approached, the nuns would have the students line up along the wall, and single-file, march out of the classroom until reaching the hallway, where two lines would be formed. Incredibly, the linoleum flooring's styling had little gold lines running down the hallways, all the way through to the cafeteria. It was every kid's duty to stay on the line's path, and not divert from it.

The nun would stand at her doorway and look up and down the hall like a traffic cop before exiting her class from her classroom. God forbid another class would be spilling out onto the hallway at the same time. The nuns wouldn't stand for such chaos. So we assembled onto our gold lines only after the hallway was absolutely safe and clear, and walked without sound to our destination with each class's nun leading the group like a drill sergeant.

Due to the lack of recess time, most boys like me who brought our lunch, would be sneaking their sandwiches out of their bags during the march to the cafeteria. When the coast was clear, I'd take a giant bite out of my baloney sandwich and chew it like a ravaged dog. We'd watch each other in amusement, seeing who could take the biggest, most jaw-deforming bite out of their sandwiches.

Once we got to the principal's office on the way to the cafeteria, it was time to check out who in the school was being punished at that time. The principal's bench along the hallway was the seat of disgrace for students. It was tantamount to being locked in a stock in the middle of the Place de Concorde, or tied to the mast of The Bounty.

Within an hour, the entire school would pass by the unfortunate victim on the principal's bench. If you knew the kid or kids on the bench, it certainly wasn't prudent to make a wisecrack or a crass sound when passing by. If a nun heard you, it wouldn't take long before you found yourself taking the kid's place on the bench of shame. Still, everybody managed to get off a goofy face or google his eyes at the imprisoned sitter.

By the time the class reached the cafeteria in single-file, I was usually jamming the final wedge of baloney sandwich into my already packed mouth. The mark of a great lunch scarfer was apparent when a kid was able to pack his cavernous pie hole with enough sandwich to enable him to simply throw his lunch bag away in the garbage can upon entering the cafeteria. This was looked upon as a prodigious achievement.

Some kids, especially the ones from richer families, didn't have the luxury of hamster-packing their sandwiches and bolting outside for an extended recess. Some had to buy their lunches in the cafeteria, which meant standing in line, paying the cashier, dragging a tray along a banquet line, and finally sitting down at an open spot in the cafeteria to chow down. This procedure cost a kid anywhere between 10 and 15 minutes of potential recess time.

Only about five or six kids per class would buy their lunch on Mondays, Wednesdays and Fridays. Mondays was the worst day to buy. It was pretty much a ripoff of 35 cents, the average lunch tab in the 1960s. The menu usually offered something like roast beef with mixed vegetables, or stew. The dessert would be something like an apple turnover or tapioca.

Wednesdays usually featured something equally unappetizing to a kid, such as brisket or ham with scalloped potatoes. Fridays were days you'd just as soon not eat at all, if you had to buy your lunch. The only reason a kid would be buying his lunch on Friday was because his mother ran out of bread for sandwiches, or, the kid lost his lunch bag on the bus or something.

At a Catholic school like I.C., you can bet your bottom dollar there wasn't going to be meat on the menu on Friday. The nuns had long made it clear to every student from the time he could scratch his own name on a sheet of paper that eating meat on Friday was a sin. A SIN! Should a slice of baloney find its way between two pieces of bread for your lunch, you were a verifiable sinner.

I never could understand what meat had to do with sinning. The common response was that it was meant to be a sacrifice, and you weren't to judge God's will. To comfort the logic, we would be reminded that Jews aren't allowed to eat pork, ever. That means no hot dogs. No barbecue ribs.

And some can't eat dairy, either! No ice cream cones! "So shut up, and finish your fish sticks, and be glad you're not Jewish!"

Certainly, our daily religion class never covered the real reason why there wasn't any meat allowed on Friday. Apparently, one of the popes hundreds of years ago decided to help the Italian fishermen sell more fish by proscribing Catholics from eating meat on Friday. As Catholic tradition generally goes, ideas become steadfast rules for centuries without any adjustment to logic.

So, thanks to an ancient pope and the lobbyists of the Italian Fishermen Federation, Immaculate Conception Grade School was serving macaroni and cheese on Friday. In those days, this wasn't a kids' favorite. It was too creamy and the pasta was mooshy. The cheese wasn't actually cheese. It was some kind of concoction derived from a yellow powder that looked like talc.

It was pretty much understood that, if you were buying your lunch on those three days, you were either a first-class dweeb or your mother had a miscarriage or something, preventing her from making your lunch.

As for me, Friday was a bad day for eating lunch anyhow. Usually, we were running out of bread at home by Friday. So, I usually could expect the butt end of the loaf of bread as one of my two slices. On top of that, my mother never believed that peanut butter and jelly was a good excuse for a kid's lunch, even on Friday, when meat was prohibited. Instead, I often found egg salad as my mother's choice on Fridays. I couldn't get her to understand that egg salad sandwiches in a kid's lunch sack looks like clam chowder between bread by the time noon rolls around. Just extricating the dripping egg salad from the plastic baggie was enough to make me toss the whole thing in the trash as soon as I entered the cafeteria.

Tuna fish sandwiches weren't a much better option, but my mother would alternate between egg and tuna as a special lunch treat.

Before throwing away my lunch on Fridays, I learned that I needed to identify what the sandwich was, first. Just in case my mother asked me that evening how I enjoyed my lunch. One time I made the mistake of complaining about the dripping gook, sending my mother into one of her patented lectures about the starving kids (who didn't have to eat egg salad for lunch) all over the world.

Once in a while, she'd make me an American cheese sandwich, which wasn't too bad. At least it was something I could cram in my mouth easily on the way to the cafeteria.

Now, the school cafeteria was quite a different place on Tuesdays and Thursdays. On those days, kids lined up at the cafeteria cashier by the dozens. It was actually quite chic to buy your lunch on either of those two days. Tuesdays always featured hamburgers and french fries. The fries were great, and the burger was so-so. Dessert was this crappy, chocolate pudding, which nobody ever ate, yet the I.C. kitchen staff never noticed—or never cared.

Yet, it was the day to buy your lunch, because everybody did. Once in a while, though, the genius who planned the menus would surprise the school with Sloppy Joes instead of hamburgers on Tuesdays. This news was always greeted with disdain, since Sloppy Joes were unwieldy sandwiches with sauce and ground hamburger dripping all over everywhere. Sloppy Joes on Tuesday was pretty much considered a dirty trick by I.C. students. We figured it was a sort of sabotaging of the lunch menu, probably because some nun preferred Sloppy Joes. The truth was, it was a kitchen steward's way of being economical, and reusing ground beef.

Thursday was a big cafeteria day usually resulting in standing room only. It was spaghetti day, and not even the principal would mess with the menu on Thursdays. After all, many of the kids in my school came from Italian families, and spaghetti was ingrained in their culture.

Besides that, the spaghetti was great. And so was the little slice of buttered, Italian bread that came with it. To us kids, the bread was like a rare delicacy, akin to the treasured little bag of peanuts on an airplane.

Immaculate Conception didn't do its spaghetti like an Italian restaurant did. They made it in trays on Wednesday, the day before, and it sat in the tomato sauce like day-old spaghetti. Well, anybody knows that spaghetti tastes even better the next day. So I.C. had its secret recipe for a great lunch—procrastinated spaghetti.

Some days, a kid would get the courage up to ask Mrs. Matiori, the kitchen matron, for an extra slice of bread. Usually the answer was, there wasn't enough to go around. But occasionally, you could mooch yourself an extra piece.

In fact, these little pieces of buttered bread were in large part the incentive for kids to work kitchen duty. Sixth-, seventh- and eighth-grade boys were enlisted to work kitchen duty throughout the year. It was hard, sweaty work, but on Thursdays, Mrs. Matiori allowed you as many pieces of bread as you wanted. Plus, you ate for free when you worked. And, best of all, you got to leave class about 25 minutes early to get to the cafeteria and begin working when the little kids arrived to eat.

Needed for kitchen duty were two tray and plate scrapers with spatulas in hand, two washers, and two stackers.

Scraping was the best job. After eating their lunch, kids, one at a time, would bring up their finished trays while the two scrapers emptied the plates and milk carton into the trash and separated the tray from the plates for the washers inside the kitchen. Scrapers always had fun chastising kids for not eating their vegetables or for not finishing their milk.

The two washers placed the plates, cups and silverware into steel racks and slid them into the conveyor-style washing machine. You sweated doing that job, but you felt like you were working in a car wash. For some reason, that seemed cool. The two stackers took the clean, steaming dining ware out of the racks and stacked everything restaurant-style for the next day.

At the end of the labor, we moseyed back to class at a snail's pace, hoping to at least miss out on something important. It was prudent not to lollygag back to class after, say, salisbury steak was on the menu. The nuns knew that the kitchen crew would be done in the cafeteria on a weak menu day easily before the start of class. Tuesday and Thursday work, however, was a legitimate reason to stumble into class as much as 10 minutes late without getting the fish-eye from a suspicious nun.

A kid only had to work in the kitchen for one week. At most, you were only asked to work in there twice a year, so it wasn't a big deal. You lost out on recess, but it was kind of a privilege at I.C. to do that kind of work. It meant you were older and more mature, although we seldom proved the latter. There were food fights and silliness going on almost always.

Joe Landry once got into a mess of trouble while doing his duty as a scraper. Inexplicably, Landry decided to slap a kid across the face with his spatula. Since he had been scraping pudding plates for the past half hour with the rubber instrument, it shouldn't have been a surprise that chocolate pudding splattered all over the victimized kid, who promptly went and tattled to Sister Ann Dominic. The rotund nun's response was to grab a spatula of her own, albeit without pudding remnants, and play a drum role on Landry's head. There were no extra Italian bread slices for him that week.

HAVING A NICE TRIP

The kitchen crew did have a chance to eat their free lunch—for about eleven seconds, which was usually long enough on most days. One day, when I was a member of the kitchen crew, I was scarfing down my food with the others at an end table when Patricia McNertny came bouncing by carrying a full lunch tray for the principal.

McNertny was one of the smart kids, but an insufferable kiss ass, volunteering her recess to assemble lunch trays and deliver them to the faculty lounge for the lazy-ass nuns.

McNertny had a penchant for walking like her legs were pogo sticks, probably because it made her brown, wavy hair bounce like the model's hair on the Prell shampoo commercials. Her head swung to the sides as it always did, all delighted in her role as the nuns' chosen schlepper.

What was about to happen elevated me to "Most Honored" status in the eyes of my classmates; more so than anything I ever did.

McNertny, hands clutched onto the stacked tray, and head a-bobbin' and hair a-breezin', managed to trip over my foot in full stride. I looked up instantly at the inadvertent foot contact, and saw McNertny, in slow motion, fly through the air with the lunch tray leading the way. She soared like Bobby Orr after he scored his famous, Stanley Cup winning goal in 1972.

I saw the expression on her face an instant after our feet met, when her brain realized there was going to be a crash landing. Her plaid skirt was flailing and her bony knees and high socks were two feet in the air, horizontal to the floor. She was flying, holding onto the tray to the bitter end. Then there was the loudest crash ever heard in the school cafeteria. The plate of spaghetti bounced off the tray, emptied its contents all over the floor then rolled on its rim like a quarter for 10 yards. The cup, once filled with hot coffee, had separated from its saucer, and both had crashed to the floor. Silverware, napkin, chocolate cake, and three pieces of buttered Italian bread were strewn over the crash site.

McNertny ended up supine on the floor, and suspiciously turned and looked at me as if I had sabotaged the whole thing.

Since the damage was already done, I didn't see any need to apologize to her or admit that I didn't do it intentionally. Besides, the roar of laughter in the cafeteria was so resounding, I decided to play this one out as McNertny's antagonist. My buddies at my table thought it was the coolest thing they'd ever seen, tripping the nun's lick ass in full flight with a tray full of grub.

My friends asked me if I, indeed, tripped her on purpose, and I answered ambiguously, saying "Who, me? Why of course not!" with a smirk and a wink.

I knew that I didn't have the courage to purposely stick out my leg and set McNertny flying while cradling a nun's lunch tray any more than I had the bravado to kiss Sister Alphonsa Marie square on the lips, Mafia-style. But I let the truth go down a different path. Besides, my now adoring classmates had someone, something to rally around. For one brief, shining moment, I was Jimmy Hoffa, having just rubbed out another victim in the name of my classmates.

By the time a host of nuns arrived to find it was only McNertny and a lunch tray that crashed instead of two Oldsmobiles, the embarrassed kid was scraping strewn spaghetti from the floor. A few kids began helping McNertny in the cleanup after the insistence of Sister Mary Barbara.

I nonchalantly drank my milk and fiddled with my food awaiting a possible on-the-spot investigation. My bravado was turning into a meek hope that McNertny wouldn't finger me as her would-be assailant. Or douse me in milk.

There was further talk about who was to blame, since this wasn't a minor incident; after all, Sister's lunch would be delayed. But McNertny never implicated me directly. I would know if she did, because the nuns would have believed her story any day of the week before mine. And they'd have crucified me for such a heinous and deliberate act.

Maybe they figured it had to be an accident since I wasn't the type of kid who had a history of doing something so despicable. Even if she fingered me, they probably laughed and said, "Who? Phillips? Ha! He's too big a chicken to do such a thing."

Anyway, I didn't get the gallows, and I maintained the notion among my classmates that maybe I did do it purposely. Nevertheless, I was grateful to McNertny for not ratting on me. Come to think of it, though, I don't think she ever gave me a valentine after that.

THE AMBUSH

Despite what the nuns probably thought of me—being a yellow-bellied coward and all, too chicken to get into serious trouble— I did cross the line one time.

One day after lunch, Womsley and I decided we'd pull a prank to end all pranks on Fred Belmarti. We were in seventh grade, and every day after lunch, it was a ritual of ours to head to the boys' room before going outside for recess.

This one day, the three of us left the cafeteria together, but Belmarti got delayed at the trash cans. Belmarti was strolling some 20 yards behind us down the hall when Womsley and I ducked into the bathroom. Together, we got the ingenious idea to ambush Fred as he entered the bathroom door, with us peeing on him from both sides. The Golden Shower!

We figured our effrontery would go unnoticed. It was a harmless prank; just another cherished I.C. memory in the making. We planned to spray him like a couple of English sheepdogs on the pants legs, and before recess was over he'd probably be dry. But what a great gag that would be, we thought. Even Belmarti could appreciate the raw lewdness of it all...after his legs dried.

So Womsley and I ducked behind the door, dropped our zippers and readied our fellows for fire. Seconds later, as planned, the door swung open, and Womsley and I turned our bladders loose, excreting a looping, steady stream as only a kid can do. We were aiming for pants legs, and that's what we got, until we realized to our horror that the kid receiving our urinary salute wasn't Belmarti. It was a sixth grader named Billy Armstead.

There couldn't have been a worse, unintentional target than Armstead. Both Womsley and I instinctively turned the waterworks off, zipped up and explained to the kid that it was all a joke, but Armstead wasn't buying it.

Then I noticed that I alone was trying to convince the kid that it was a prank, and not intended for him. I looked around, and Womsley had slyly ducked around the corner in the bathroom, out of site. As Armstead raged, "I saw you peeing on the floor!" I realized that I was in deep trouble. And my accomplice maybe was getting away with this whole thing unidentified.

While I beckoned with Armstead to listen to reason, he asserted that he was going to tell Sister.

The kid starts walking back toward the cafeteria while I followed him, beseeching him not to do any such thing.

But his mind was made up. He kept repeating, "I'm gonna tell Sister! I saw you peeing on the floor! You was peeing on the floor, and I saw you! I'm going to tell Sister."

I gave up my chase of him and headed back into the bathroom where Womsley was hiding behind a locker wall. We both started laughing; the kind of nervous laugh you have when you know you're about to die.

Then Womsley blurted out, "Where the hell did Belmarti go!" We both dashed out of the bathroom and headed outside for the playground. We never saw Belmarti. He vanished. Or maybe he turned into Armstead.

As we bolted for a hiding place among the crowd of recessing kids, Womsley and I discussed our predicament.

"Whatta ya think they'll do to us?" I asked him. "Are you kidding?" he responded hopelessly. "For pissing on another kid in the bathroom? We pissed on the floor, too, you know!"

"Christ, we're dead, man," I analyzed. "What the fuck do we do now?" (Four-letter words of this variety were common among us by the seventh grade. After all, we'd caddied the entire summer, and the lexicon at the caddyshack required a kid to be casually bilingual.)

"We can't let them find us together on the playground," Womsley figured. "Let's scram."

We headed up to the upper level of the playground, where construction workers were putting the finishing touches on the new church. We stalled around the parked trucks a while, then doubled around the school and entered through the front entrance of the classroom school. Since recess was still under way, we ducked into the second floor boys' room and looked out the window toward the playground.

There we saw Sister Daniel Marie being led by Armstead up the road toward the playground, obviously intent on pointing us out to the sour-pussed nun. The way they were walking, they were looking for someone. And we knew who.

"Holy shit!" Womsley exclaimed. "They're looking for us! We're screwed, buddy. Big time!"

As I thought about the impending torture that the nuns would inflict upon us, a new, more pernicious problem came to mind.

"Hey! Goddammit! Armstead's black!" I shouted.

"Huh?" grunted Womsley, questioning the relevance of the observation.

"He's black, he's black! Jesus Christ, Tugboat might figure we were pissing on him because he's black!"

Womsley's jaw dropped, and his eyebrows rose. HIs eyes glazed over in fear. He never thought of that. After all, this was the '60s. Late '60s. White people weren't pissing on Blacks anymore, literally or figuratively. Except for in Alabama. And this wasn't Alabama!

Purposely pissing on the floor in Catholic School in an attempt to douse a classmate—who wasn't even on fire—could be perceived by a nun as truly Satan-inspired.

Now, add to the scenario two boys ostensibly choosing to take a whiz, ambush-style, on an unsuspecting, younger black kid. Not only that, this kid, Armstead, is a big-for-his-age, shy, gentle type who wouldn't hurt a fly. And no fly with a conscience would hurt him, either.

"Son-of-a-bitch, Tugboat will find us in no time," I claimed, acknowledging Sister Daniel Marie by her student-given name. "Wait a minute, does Armstead know you? He's pretty much a new kid..."

"Uh-uh. I don't think so. He knows my brother, but I don't think he knows me. Besides, I don't know if he got a good look at me."

"Yeah, you ducked out of way while I was pleading with him!" I readied to slug Womsley in the arm for the desertion when he had a brainstorm.

'Listen, let's change sweaters. He might not be able to identify you in my sweater. Switching sweaters might fuck him up."

"You think? Hey, do white kids look alike to black kids?" I asked, as serious as hell, hoping being a homogeneous white kid would help camouflage us in a jungle of lily-white students.

We slipped off our sweaters and exchanged them. Through the bathroom window, we watched the kid with the wet pants legs lead the warden-like nun on a search of the playground for us two fugitives.

"Where the hell did Belmarti go?" quizzed Womsley one last time.

"He fuckin' vanished, that's where..."

Womsley started to figure our plan. "The good thing is, nobody else saw us, right? It's his word against ours. If he fingers us, we'll say we weren't even in the bathroom at lunchtime."

"Right. Listen, we'll say you and I weren't even together during lunch at all. You say you were with Belmarti. Even Fred doesn't know what the hell happened. I'll say I was at the lost and found looking for my sweater, or something. That way, if someone notices we're wearing a different sweater, I'll say I found mine in the lost and found."

Womsley agreed. We waited for the recess bell to ring, then melted into our class's line to head back to the room.

That afternoon we sweat it out, literally and figuratively. Not only did we fear Armstead picking us out of a classroom lineup, but also, we both had to wear each other's sweater the rest of the day. After all, the sweaters were our only disguise, and we had to wear them in case Armstead should appear with a nun in tow to do a once over of our classroom, looking for suspects.

We waited. And watched the clock. And waited. Each class went by at an excruciatingly slow pace. The back of my neck was sweaty the entire day. When finally the bell rang to end school, Womsley and I surreptitiously slipped out of the classroom, wondering if the next day would bring an inquisition.

The next day came and went, as did the weeks and months. We never heard a thing about the incident. No scuttlebutt. No rumors. No discernible sign from the nuns that they were on a witchhunt.

The whole thing blew over, but to be sure, Womsley and I never went down that same hallway to the bathroom again after lunch. We took the main hallway, like most of the others, in the event the nuns were casing the scene of the "crime." After all, even we knew that stupid crooks are eventually seen going back to the scene of the crime. Well, we might have been guilty, but we weren't stupid. We wore halos the rest of the year just in case the nuns were secretly investigating. To this day, neither Womsley nor I have ever pissed on another student. We learned our lesson.

Our tackle pom pom field, years later, now a corral for pre-schoolers.

KILLER MARROO

I was always thankful to God that I wasn't a girl. I could never figure out what the hell they did for recess. Once they became too old to play on the teeter tauter, swings or the merry-go-round, or take their turn going down the slide, their life was just about over, as far as I could see.

Girls hadn't really been encouraged to play sports in the days of the 1960s, so the ones that did were considered tomboys. Most girls tried to avoid that moniker. So their recess time was pretty much relegated to kicking a pebble around in a circle or joining the goddam choir.

Since the school's pastor, Monsignor James Murphy, didn't much believe in sports, the school's superb gymnasium went to waste. There were no sports teams for the kids to participate in—no football, no basketball (despite the beautiful gym) no baseball, no tennis. There were no clubs, either. Somehow, extracurricular activities, aside from attending Mass, were frowned upon at I.C. There was no confusing this place with a country club.

Immaculate Conception's playground consisted of the upper level parking area up by the new church, the lower level parking area behind the school, the younger children's area of monkey bars and swings, and a stretch of grass that was encompassed by classrooms in an L shape.

This stretch of grass was known by all students as the tackle pom pom field. Every day, Immaculate Conception boys blew off steam on this mini rugby field during recess by playing tackle pom pom.

I've seen films of kids in poor countries like Russia, China and Brazil kicking a hand-made sack of rags shaped like a soccer ball around a yard and calling it a game.

Well, we at Immaculate Conception didn't even have rags to make a ball. Not that we were poor. There weren't any balls on the playground. Ever. They didn't allow balls. I think the nuns felt that, since a ball wasn't actually a religious artifact, it had no place at Immaculate Conception. After all, there were no records in the Bible of Jesus ever playing ball. Nowhere in The Scriptures does it read, "And Jesus said to his second baseman, you take the relay throw, I'll take the base." Did Jesus ever hang around with Matthew and Mark tossing a football around while discussing the Romans?

There's no record that Jesus even believed in recess, so we didn't press the issue.

We had to invent a game without a prop of any kind. What evolved was I.C.'s version of tackle pom pom, also known as "Killer Marroo."

Pom pom at other schools besides I.C. was a game where kids lined up on one side of a field, and one person remained in the middle of the field. Upon saying "pom pom," the herd of kids tried to make it to the other side of the field without being tagged by the kid in the middle.

If you were tagged, you joined the kid in the middle in pursuit of the rest of the kids who would run back again at the called signal of "pom pom."

Before long, the majority of kids get caught and end up pursuing the minority, until one final kid is left to be caught by the rest.

Now, that's the way the rest of the schools played Pom Pom. At I.C., there was far too much frustration brewing in the craniums of the kids to settle for such an innocuous version of a ball-less playground game.

Pom pom was euphemistically called "tackle pom pom" by the kids, but the truth is, the game was a cross between rugby and "assault with the intent to kill."

It took guts to play I.C. pom pom, and I was surprised that so many boys joined in the fray. It was physical, even brutal at times. Kids including myself got creamed with flying elbows, beheaded by "clothesline" swings, smashed with forearm shivers, and body slammed to the turf like mannequins.

Some kids enjoyed being pursued, others preferred being the pursuer. I liked both. I was a pretty shifty runner and a devastating tackler. It was fun to lay some of my Gale Sayers-like moves out on the field, leaving would-be tacklers grasping at the air. But inevitably, the numbers were too much to outrun. Looking ahead and seeing 20 kids preparing to bear down on you at the call of "pom pom" was a humbling experience. I just put my head down and tried to bowl over a kid or two before being piled on by a dozen gouging opponents.

I had my favorite strategies for tackling unsuspecting runners. Having noticed how lions bring down their prey in a scurrying herd, I liked to cut across the grain of traffic at a full run and blindside an unsuspecting kid trotting north. It was easy to send a kid heels over elbows with a crackback jolt out of nowhere. What a great feeling that was, too; to smash a good friend of yours like he was a fleeing bank robber, or something.

One day I caught Ben Clack, the tallest kid in our class, skipping his way to the other end, thinking the coast was clear. With his head turned back over his right shoulder, I blindsided him from the left, sending his long, lanky appendages sprawling and tumbling to the ground. He went down like windmill in a tornado.

It was particularly fun to be the first tackler on the field. Most first tacklers chose the weakest kids to bring down in order to build the number of tacklers in the middle.

I preferred to pick out the biggest, toughest kid right from the start. That usually meant I'd isolate on Landry or Ralston or Lorrenzo like a lion picking out his prey. At the call of "pom pom," the other kids would whisk by, clicking their heels and frolicking to the end of the field without having any heed paid to them. When Landry realized he was the target, he'd try everything to escape, since the whole playground was watching this one-on-one battle.

Landry was built like a Coke machine. There was no way to get your arms around him. He had to be taken down by the legs. He usually was tackled by a dozen kids who climbed on him like a tree before finally timbering him over. But on this day, Landry was going to go down at the hands of one kid—a kid half his size—me.

With two dozen of my peers watching behind me, I charged forward in a suicide collision course with the eighth grade's toughest kid. Nobody had ever challenged Landry one on one in pom pom. He was a runner whose demise could be prudently postponed until an army was assembled to negotiate him to the turf.

But not today. This was the day Landry was going to learn that he can be taken. The field was leveling out. No more dominance. One kid wasn't afraid to take him on, head to head.

I wasn't afraid of getting hurt since every day we all got hurt to some degree playing the game. Pain had long been an accepted consequence of tackle pom pom. And if Landry powered over me, so what, that's what everyone was expecting anyhow. So if he stomped me into the ground, I figured I'd get up and demolish one of the smaller kids in retribution, anyhow. I was going to punish someone. My first choice—my dream—was to cream Landry. If that failed, my back-up plan was to decapitate the elfish Rickie Harrison.

Once I had Landry in my sights, he trotted to the left, and I followed. Then he drifted back to the right until he saw I would cut off his escape either way.

Then he did exactly what I expected. Landry put his ears back, lowered his head and charged forward like a buffalo, heavy legs churning and left forearm cocked to deliver a Jim Brown-like bolo blow.

Landry gritted his teeth and prepared to run through me like a mulberry bush. In a deranged state of mind, I lowered my head and charged forward like Bambi gone mental.

No physics professor could explain what happened next. Landry's weight—all 190 pounds of him—was levered forward. At the speed he was running, he could have toppled over a bus. But I hit him low and hard, right in the mid section. My shoulder buried in his sternum as the wind escaped his lungs like a burst balloon. His body's momentum instantly went limp as my impetus continued forward. With the big kid out of air and hunched over my back, I drove him onto his back and landed on top, driving him into the turf. As he looked skyward, gasping for air, I continued to crawl over the top of him, raking my forearm across his face, turning his cheek into the ground. For added emphasis, I popped to my feet, dusted my hands over the sprawled Landry, and all but beat my chest in Tarzan fashion.

As Landry shook the cobwebs out of his head and began to get up, I realized that I may have bitten off more than I could chew.

Yes, I had just proved that David indeed could beat Goliath—once. My growing fear now was that Landry was about to prove that, nine out of 10 falls, Goliath obliterates David.

As the rest of the playground buzzed about the violent tackle applied to Landry, I wondered about my personal safety.

I extended my hand to help Landry to his feet, hoping he'd remember the friendship that we'd shared for nine years. He brushed my hand aside and jumped to his feet. Needing to do something to recover his dominance, Landry started laughing and poking me. Finally he stepped on my foot—an old boxer's trick—and pushed me to the ground. Laughing, he called me a bastard, helped me up, and we turned our joint attention to demolishing the rest of the runners.

It was amazing that the nuns allowed us to play our "Killer Marroo" during recess. Every day, somebody after recess seemed to come back to class bleeding. There were plenty of grass-stained shirts, torn pockets, and stretched out ties.

The nuns certainly could see us from the classroom windows. I guess they liked watching the violence. They couldn't stand the thought of us talking or chewing gum, but clotheslining a fellow student on the pom pom field apparently appealed to them. If any one of those nuns could have hiked up their long, black habits and kicked off those thick-heeled clodhoppers they wore, they could have had a good time out on the playground. It seemed like their kind of fun.

Some days, after listening to a nun's tirade in class, I would close my eyes and dream, envisioning her lined up on the pom pom field. Just her and me, and my 20 or so classmates. All at once, we shout "pom pom" in unison, and the nun charges forward. And we all tackle her like a blocking dummy, one at a time. When she gets up, the next guy clobbers her. Then the next guy. Then the next.

What a dream! It brings a tear to my eye.

Sorry, Sister! You must not have heard my horn!

CHOIR—FUN FOR NUNS

Sister Mary Barbara had the brilliant idea one year to encourage both girls and boys of the eighth grade to sing in the choir. She felt that good students would volunteer their recess to participate in the choir practice.

Most of the girls volunteered without any reservations since Sister Mary Barbara was their teacher, for one, and two, girls didn't have much to do at recess, anyhow. Besides, one thing was clear about volunteering for anything Sister Mary Barbara suggested: your volunteering was mandatory.

The boys felt the pressure, too, so most of us capitulated. The good thing about practicing for the choir during recess was that we finally had a chance to be in the same room as the girls, even if separated across the room.

All nuns seemed to carry little, round, black pitch pipes with them. These pocket-sized harmonicas in the round were a favorite devise of nuns who were making themselves seem like musicians. They would blow a note, but would never explain to us what the hell that sound meant.

Certainly we were supposed to begin in that key. But we were such lousy singers, we had no idea how to match that sound or when to match that sound.

Most of the boys were lousy singers, and I was among the worst. The biggest reason why I couldn't sing was because I didn't want to sing. Most of the boys fell into this category. Reluctant participants.

Sister Mary Barbara would walk around the room with her music book open, thrusting her ear unsuspectingly next to your mouth to see if you were singing.

It was a well-known practice to mouth the words silently until Mary Barbara got close. Sometimes I'd wait too long to sound off, and the crackle of my suddenly starting-up singing voice would give away my muteness. While the singing continued, Mary Barbara would chastise any person for not singing loud enough.

It was most important to every nun that your singing included the perfect "O" shape of your mouth. The nuns even had a drill for us to practice so that our goddam mouths would emit singing sounds while shaped like an "O".

"Nnnnneeeeeewwwwwwwwww-ooooohhh-hhhhhh-Aaaaa hhhhhhhhhh" We repeated this mouth-rounding sound like it was the Gregorian Chant, for chrissake, over and over and over again.

It never failed. The nuns could even sap the fun out of music.

SEXUAL SEGREGATION

The nuns, sociopaths as they were, believed that boys and girls in the seventh and eighth grades needed to be separated at all times. Therefore, they stuck us in separate classrooms. Mary Barbara took the girls, and Alphonsa Marie had the boys.

To better prepare us for high school, the nuns thought it was authentic to have the boys and girls swap classrooms twice a day. So, the nuns stood in the middle of the hallway, patrolling the two lines of kids passing each other, making sure no students made eye contact with the opposite sex.

"Keep your eyes on your neighbor ahead of you," they'd bark.

"Something interesting, Mr. Keshawn? You better watch where you're going, big boy."

"Don't look at me, big boy! Look straight ahead!"

Thanks to the nuns, any kid coming out of Immaculate Conception had a lot of catching up to do with the opposite gender. They had a way of making a boy feel guilty for being interested in a girl. Or just looking at one. The nuns could only understand abstinence when it came to relating to others. They saw boys and girls as two different animals that needed to be kept in separate cages, like lions and hyenas.

This belief of the nuns was never more clearly driven home than on the day of Immaculate Conception's Eighth Grade trip. While other schools send their Eighth Graders to Washington, D.C. for an educational, three-day excursion, Immaculate Conception's idea of a memorable experience was to take the Eighth Grade to Chicago. The Second City was not a novel idea, since we were living in a suburb just 25 miles north.

The nuns' plan? Wizz us through the city in two buses—on a Saturday! We didn't even miss any school. The mandatory class trip began in the school parking lot at 8 a.m. The nuns piled the girls into one bus, and the boys on the other. Since there wasn't room enough for five girls on their bus, they had to ride with the boys.

When the boys found out about five girls riding along with us during the trip, there was an excitement in the air. Maybe the trip wouldn't be as dull as promised. That optimism died quickly as the five girls boarded our bus.

The nuns had carefully handpicked the five girls to ride with the boys. Each girl was a sure bet to grow up and become either a spinster or a nun.

On that Eighth Grade trip to Chicago, we breezed by Chinatown like it was a gap-toothed hitchhiker. That part of town was one of the highlights, supposedly, on the trip's itinerary.

We stopped at a roller rink. Had our bagged lunch. Then we went to the Prudential Building's observation deck on the 50th floor, but the condensation from the day's rain made the windows opaque.

We ate dinner in near silence at some steak restaurant, and went back to school—a typically disastrous nun-run affair.

LEARNING THE CATHOLIC GUILT

One thing the nuns did an excellent job at was beating religion into your brain. Every day, school began at the bell with catechism. No matter what grade we were in, we had a religion book and a workbook that we'd fill out with answers to every type of question imaginable about Roman Catholicism. The nuns certainly knew their material. They also had a penchant for adding their own interpretations. Often times, it was apparent that the nuns could read God's mind, knowing exactly what He deemed good and bad. They always were sure of what constituted an eternity in Hell, too.

The very first thing you learned in kindergarten was that if a kid missed Mass on Sunday or any Holy Day of Obligation, you were in violation of one of God's most stringent rules, and thereby destined for infinite eons in Hell. One day missed and you were Hell-bound forever. That's the nuns' interpretation of their God's logic. In fact, this was merely the nuns' logic. There's still hope that God is a tad more judicial in His thinking.

The nuns at I.C. used fear as their most powerful, pedagogical motivator. There was no better way to insure 100 percent attendance at Mass than to put the fear of the Lord's everlasting revenge in a child's heart.

The nuns always taught that Jesus loves you. We heard it all the time. Jesus loves YOU. He loves ALL children. Except, of course, if you're a no-show at collection time during Sunday's Mass. Then, he'll slam the Gates of Heaven in your face like you were a tambourine-tapping Hari-Kristna.

You knew to look both ways—twice—when crossing the street after having missed Mass on Sunday. That speeding bus coming at you just might have Jesus behind the wheel, angry as hell, looking to take you out.

It always was disturbing to me that Confessions were held on Fridays at Immaculate Conception, a long and treacherous five days after Sunday. That meant you had to be extra careful with your life until you could blab your mortal sin of missing Mass out to Monsignor Murphy or Father Garbin, the executors of God's will.

There was no component of being Catholic that I disliked more than Confession. The nuns taught that a good Catholic should be at confession once a week, conveying his sins to a priest, who serves as God's earthly liaison. Once a week!

The nuns believed that people were sinning virtually every day of their lives. Even pious people. Even the conscripted kids attending Immaculate Conception. Sinning constantly. The nuns made us feel like we were whirling dervishes of sin.

The classic example of a nun showing a kid his evil ways happened to me at the hands of Sister Agnes Marita in fifth grade.

Of all the nuns I've encountered, Sister Agnes Marita was the one I liked most—or disliked the least. Yet, probably no other kid at I.C. would share this same affection for her.

Agnes Marita was a tall, Texan-accented woman with dark shadows under her eyes. She was nicknamed "Lurch" after the towering, ghoulish butler on the Addams Family TV show.

You didn't mess with the long, tall Texan. She could send a shiver up your spine just by folding her arms and peering down at you with that intimidating scowl of hers. When she got pissed, she'd raise her eyebrows and laser beam a hole through you with her mysteriously scary eyes.

She threatened kids all the time with the same refrain, "I'll slap you over!" Yet, I don't recall her ever laying a glove on a kid.

The statuesque nun would stride down the hallway, almost always with her arms folded in front of her, seldom moving her head. Often times, I'd passed her in the hallway and offer an obligatory "Good morning, Sister," only to be answered silently by her crookedly suspicious grin.

To a lesser-trained eye, the angular nun seemed to be a difficult, brooding, misanthrope—like most nuns at I.C.

After a while, I figured her out. She was like a tootsie pop. Hard shell on the outside, soft and chewy in the center. She was all facade, playing the tough nun; loud, Doberman bark with the bite of a goldfish.

But I didn't figure that out until the seventh grade. In fifth grade, she nailed me. I had forgotten the nun-professed postulate that we all are sinners. Constantly!

During Christian Doctrine class, Sister Agnes Marita decided to take a survey with a show of hands from the class. I sat in the second row and the second seat on this day. The embarrassment won't let me forget.

"How many in this room feel they haven't sinned in a month?" asked the nun.

I quickly shot up my hand in response, thinking the nun was going to continue the questioning with "Two months? A year?" But there were no further questions.

Way too late to reverse my silent declaration, I noticed that my hand was the only one in the air.

The giant nun turned her head slowly and suspiciously toward me, then peered at me with an elevated eyebrow.

Then she uttered sarcastically yet comically in her Texan twang, "Well, Mr. Phillips, we're gonna have to erect a statue of you in the new church!"

As I lowered my hand, the class laughed heartily at my lack of sin awareness.

The irony of it all wasn't lost on me, even in the fifth grade. Only in Catholic School could a kid feel guilty for not feeling guilty.

THE PRIESTS

As foolish as it sounds, the nuns were pretty much in step with the religion itself. After all, if you're a Catholic, you are born with "Original Sin," a black mark on your soul that comes with your first breath on Earth.

According to the theologians of Roman Catholicism, a tour of the maternity ward in any hospital would be a showcase of all the brand new sinners introduced into the world. Each infant was smitten with Original Sin, a malignant, religion gene inherited from Adam and Eve.

This Original Sin can only be absolved by being baptized. That's how the religion hooks you in right from the get-go. No parents want to be guilty of risking their children's eternal future by ignoring the first Sacrament of Baptism. According to the nuns' teaching, a person who doesn't get baptized and dies goes to Limbo, a void of a place, forever. No paradise. No hula girls. No mai-tais with little umbrellas. Eternal emptiness. And how do the nuns know this? They know all, so why ask.

I wondered how in the world they expected us to get any sins going while we're imprisoned at our desks five days a week, and at Mass on Sunday.

The nuns explained that even our thoughts were sins. Bad thoughts were evil, and sins in the eyes of God. That didn't bode well for me or anyone else I knew at I.C. We had bad thoughts about the nuns all the time. I can't remember many times seeing a nun walking down the stairs without hoping she'd trip on her rosary beads and do a double gainer.

But, under which category did impure thoughts fall? The nuns went along with the 10 Commandments. Those were the sins you had to worry about. The mortal ones. The rest were supposed to be venial sins, I thought. But the nuns didn't buy that. For example, if you did a shitty job on your math homework one night, that could be a venial sin, according to the nuns. If you came to class without your homework and said your dog ate it, that was a lie—a mortal sin.

They always led you to believe that your interpretation of a venial sin may in fact be a mortal sin in God's eyes. Only He knows. Therefore, you better clear it all up in Confession. By the way, it might lightning out tonight, so you better get to Confession early.

Three priests conducted Confessions at Immaculate Conception on Friday nights. This was most convenient for all those Catholics who wouldn't dream of going out on a Friday night, but rather concentrate on absolving their wickedness for another week.

The surly Monsignor Murphy was the head of the parish, and God only knows who gave him the distinction of monsignor. He was about 65 years old—his entire life, as best I could tell. He had no use for kids whatsoever. Never saw him attempt to gain a rapport with a kid in nine years that I attended his school and parish.

Murf the Surf was the poster priest for Judaism. If he's a Catholic, then that's reason enough to be a Jew. One could reason that any religion that Murphy embraced had to be a wrong choice. That's how powerful an influence he was on people. He was as repulsive as an electron is to a proton.

Father Garbin was a middle-aged guy who was round like the Earth. Not perfectly round, but with a bit more bulge in the center than at the poles. Garbin had to be 400 pounds if he was an ounce. When he walked, he actually waddled. But he wasn't a bad guy. He could actually talk to a kid and make him feel that he cared.

The trouble with Garbin was, whenever he talked to you or to the entire class, he punctuated every sentence with an annoying "Huh?"

Once a week, our religion class was treated to a cameo appearance by either Murf the Surf or Garbin.

Every kid preferred Garbin because at least he wasn't a grumpy old bastard. But after five minutes of listening to him, all the class could do was count all the "Huh's" he'd grunt out.

"It's important to go to Mass, huh. Isn't it, huh. You need to pray, huh. And talk to God, huh. 'Cause he's the Savior, huh, huh, huh. He died for your sins, huh, huh..."

After 20 minutes of listening to Garbin rabble on, you wanted to stand up and scream, "Shut the fuck up already with the 'huhs,' will ya!"

After every Garbin visit, the kids sarcastically would walk around grunting at each other, "huh, huh" after every mock sentence. "Hey, I'm Father Garbin, huh, huh. You got a cream puff? Huh, huh. How 'bout a banana split, huh, huh."

Murphy, on the other hand, was a walking black hole of reverse energy. He could sap the energy out of the air quicker than a flash fire. Never saw the old grump smile, ever. He looked as if he'd rather be anywhere then where he was at, no matter where he was. That's how he inspired us kids, too. If Murphy was the embodiment of what the Church saw as a leader of its religion, it must be one, whacked organization.

The Surf was a growler of a talker. He didn't have a normal voice, but rather a throaty, gargling allocution. Everybody imitated his mumbling, gravely voice, and in order to do it, you had to shift your jaw and talk out of the side of your mouth, like Popeye.

When a nun would announce that Monsignor Murphy was joining our catechism class today, an inaudible groan could be felt rippling through the rows of desks and chairs. Twenty minutes of listening to Murphy should have been enough penance paid to release a thousand wayward souls from Purgatory. Maybe even a few from the depths of Hell. He was the embodiment of ennui. After 30 minutes of Murphy, a kid would prefer smashing himself repeatedly in the head with his catechism book, in monk-like fashion.

Every quarter at the end of the grading session, Murphy would attend each class and hand out the report cards, one at a time to the kids. It was such a disgraceful joke watching and listening to this old bastard read off the names of kids whose parents have been in the parish for years and years.

He'd read off the name on the report card and mispronounce every name that had more than two syllables. Then he'd open the card and look over the grades, then stare at you as you walked to the front of the classroom to retrieve it.

"Marsha Nishay" (for Nitsche). "Johnny Reknow (for Renoir). Mark Ventura (for Venturosi). "Jessica Monticello" (for Montribello), "Mary De Gratzi" (De Grazen).

At least to his credit, Murf seldom opened his trap about a kid's grades. Maybe once or twice he'd grumble how Pasqualoni needed to get on the ball, or Ralston needed to do better. He may have growled out a "Good" to Cynthia Keaton or a "Fine" to Sharon Payton, but he was basically a blank for the rest of the class.

When I got called up, he'd hand it to me like he never saw me before. He'd take a peak at the nun's assessment of my work, and hand it to me like it was a water bill.

REPORT CARDS—A TIME OF HUMILITY

My report cards never changed from one semester to the next. I was a classic C to B guy in the eyes of the nuns. I was an excellent speller, but almost never managed more than a B by the end of the grading period.

The nuns gave so many tests and quizzes, that it was very difficult to maintain an A average for an entire grading period. Especially when Catholic schools found it necessary to grade their kids on another scale than public kids.

In any public school, a grade of 92 was a strong A. But not at Immaculate Conception. The same grade of 92 brought only a B to an I.C. student's report card. And you can believe that a nun wasn't going to give the "A" nod to an average of 92. 93 to 100 was an A. A "B" was 85 to 92; a "C" was

77 to 84. A kid was nailed with an ignominious "D" even with the grade average of 76, a high C in public school. If you got below a 70 average, you flunked!

Relatively speaking, if you missed three questions on a 10 question quiz, you were borderline flunking! In public school, that same result made you borderline "C." That's a big difference in the way your parents felt about your effort, not the mention a student's own morale.

The right side of the report card was reserved for grading behavior. The categories were Effort, Conduct, Homework, and School Spirit. An "A" in Effort was described in the footnote as "Outstanding—maximum use of talent." My score usually was "B," "Commendable, steady effort to improve." The typical nun grade was "C,' Satisfactory. "Does required work, nothing more."

I always got straight "B's" in Conduct. "Has broken some school rules, but is improving." The nuns considered sharpening your pencil when the bell rings an infraction of a school rule. I guess if you did enough mea culpas, you were improving.

The description for an "A" in Homework read, "Does independent study in addition to assigned homework." So, by I.C.'s standards, if you were currently working on your thesis in sixth grade, you would receive an "A" in Homework.

School Spirit was the most suspect of all categories. In order to achieve an "A," you had to satisfy the following legend description: "Enthusiastically and generously participates in extracurricular projects." I allege that there were virtually no school events in which to participate. No sports teams. No plays. No after-school clubs. I think Patricia McNertny cornered the market in School Spirit by creating her lunch tray delivery service for nuns in the faculty lounge. Other than that service, earning an "A" in School Spirit was impossible.

The left side of the report card itemized the subjects: Christian Doctrine, English, Reading, Spelling, Handwriting, Arithmetic, History, Geography, Science, Music and Art.

All nuns were well versed in Christian Doctrine, and they all knew how to pound home the Word of the Lord. Most nuns and the few I.C. lay teachers were very skilled at teaching English and Reading. Spelling and Vocabulary were strong suits at I.C., too.

When it came to Music, we were talking about church hymns only. Art was handled by an obscure teacher hired as a general contractor, I think. It consisted of scribbling chalk onto large pieces of paper in the hopes of showing contrast or dimension. I can't remember having any fun or learning anything in Art class, although it certainly was a welcomed break from having to look at a black-shrouded nun all day.

History by definition wasn't anything the nuns liked to deal with since sooner or later controversy about religion would surface. Science! Forget it. That's exactly what the nuns did. Forget it! Science class was always held on Fridays. One day a week. Science would be postponed whenever possible. Virtually anything superseded it. Friday Mass, fire drill, birthday party, assembly... anything but science. Nuns hated it.

Certainly no nun wanted to get into the deep questions of the universe, the origins of Earth, or the machination of the Solar System. We're talking about old-school nuns who were products of pre-historic teachings; that God himself created the universe in six days. And, in perfect human reasoning, rested the seventh day. After all, you'd be tired too if you did all that in just six days.

Further, all nuns believed and taught that two of every type of creature on Earth was comfortably organized onto a single Ark in the antediluvian days during the Biblical flood. They never questioned the enormity of that feat, considering that they themselves couldn't even get English-speaking I.C. kids to line up double-file after Mass on Fridays.

Staunch Catholics, and nuns in particular, don't like science when it flies in the face of thousands of years of scripture or lore. The nuns, and the Vatican particularly, prefer miracles. It's miracles that enable a simple do-gooder to reach saintly status.

One of the prerequisites for attaining sainthood is the performance of three miracles. The Vatican looks very carefully at this category. Two miracles don't cut it. Has to be three. Don't try lobbying your favorite martyr unless he's packing three miracles. After all, almost anybody can come up with one or two miracles. It's that third miracle that separates the saints from the ain'ts.

It's clear to me that if Siegfried and Roy were born a mere 800 years earlier, their body remains would be relics implanted within altars all over the world. Can you imagine how the scriptures would have read eight centuries ago after the famed magicians made the Sphinx disappear? Move over, St. Aloisius.

An ancient-born Kreskin could have been immortalized as a saintly icon after three spectacular card tricks, for chrissakes.

I've always wondered how many ahead-of-their time prestidigitators attained their required three miracles for sainthood through legerdemain rather than divine intervention. Hell, I'll bet that the entire hillside of villagers were incredulous the first time they saw a sophist yank a rabbit out of his hat.

Science class was like the worst TV show in the Neilson ratings. It could get bumped from the schedule in a second's notice.

I remember Sister Agnes Marita calling off science class one Friday because Kevin O'Brien forgot to bring a string for his lab experiment. The nun's heart was never into the subject, and either was O'Brien's. In defense of the absent-minded kid, however, it wasn't easy to remember three weeks back when the last science class was held.

In desperation to save himself from a failing grade, O.B. tried to make due with a thread from his freshly torn sock. The nun would have none of it. It was the perfect excuse for her to feign disgust and cancel the class.

To me, nuns could turn Steven Seagal into a cry baby.

PUNISHMENT OVER REWARD

At I.C., it was always about the threat of doing poorly, never the reward for doing well. After being in the school for years, you became type cast. A nun could do her report cards on the first day of school for the entire year, if she wanted. Maybe that's how they did it, for all I know. It wouldn't surprise me.

It was the school's inherent policy to teach by the punishment method, as opposed to the reward method. The Socratic method wasn't even considered, since the nuns' style of teaching predated Socrates.

You paid attention. Otherwise, you got smacked. You did your homework. Otherwise, you were punished. Points were deducted from your work, never accrued. Incentives were never introduced into the teaching strategy at Immaculate Conception. Reverse incentive was based on the premise that if you did poorly, bad things would happen.

There were no incentives at Immaculate Conception, only repercussions. Once, a nun actually tried to install an incentive program into her classroom, but it failed miserably, of course.

I'll never forget Sister Michael Ann announce that there would be a classroom spelling bee every other Friday. Kids loved spelling bees. One, it was fun to stand up at the front of the class. When it was your turn, you had your 15 seconds of fame as you spelled out the nun's chosen word for you. If you were right, you hung around the blackboard in a line. If you were wrong, you sat down and watched the gradual disappearance of spellers.

I wanted to win a spelling bee so badly, I could taste it. But I never did. The best I did was hang around to the final four or five, but for some reason, I was never in the money.

I don't know if I was a choker, or what. Seemed like I always got a word like "impostor," which few non-lexicographers realize is spelled with two "o's." Or "segue," which I never even knew the meaning of, let alone could imagine was spelled out the way it is.

If you were a gambler, you'd put your money on Ellen Mallory or John Sarducci or maybe Cynthia

Keaton for the spelling bee. Patricia McNertny or Janet Mahoney were dark horses. Michael Banyon a long shot. The rest of the kids were pretty much off the chart, thousand to one shots.

One thing you knew for sure, the nuns didn't have the sense to give a stupider kid an easier word at first to build his confidence a little. Hell no. Sister Michael Ann, the spelling bee conductor, would gift-wrap the word "wonderful" on Sarducci, and hit brain-dead Pomeroy with "sesquipedalian."

I remember Sister Michael Ann proclaim that there would be a spelling bee prize—a holy card. Now one might assume that this is quite a measly prize for winning a spelling bee, defeating 30 other kids in sudden-death elimination. But to I.C. kids, a holy card was quite a prize. It was the first incentive I could ever remember being offered at I.C.

I had never won a holy card, and never knew anyone else who'd received one as a reward, either. You'd think holy cards were a dime a dozen in a Catholic school like I.C. The assumption would be, they dish out holy cards as bookmarks. Every kid must have more Francis of Assisi holy cards than he has Warren Spahn baseball cards.

It just wasn't so. In nine years of Catholic School, I never got a holy card—except when my aunt died. And that was at another church.

The spelling bee was my chance. Any prize being handed out by Immaculate Conception nuns was tantamount to receiving a Pulitzer or Nobel prize. I set my sights on winning a spelling bee, and proudly presenting it to my parents as proof of my unheralded excellence.

Then Sister explained the caveat. The holy card wouldn't be obtained merely by winning a single spelling bee. A student had to win FIVE spelling bees—FIVE!—in order to come away with the holy card.

Even in the fifth grade, I realized how incredibly parsimonious this proclamation was. There was no way a kid could win five times. With a spelling bee every other week, there wasn't enough weeks to hold spelling bees. Not to mention that more often than not, the spelling bees were postponed. Either First Friday Mass preempted the spelling bee, or the event was cancelled as punishment for the class being noisy that day. Or, there wasn't any school that Friday due to a teacher's meeting or something.

In all, Sister Michael Ann proctored over eleven or twelve spelling bees during the year.

Ellen Mallory won three times, a prodigious achievement in any kid's eyes, considering one had to spell up to 10 or 12 rather difficult words perfectly, under pressure. Still, for all her spelling prowess, even Ellen Mallory didn't win a goddam, precious holy card.

THE CURLY SHUFFLE

Whenever the routine of "sit down, open your book, close your mouth, and pay attention" was broken, the students at Immaculate Conception gave thanks. First Fridays of every month provided us with the much-awaited diversion from the drudgery of nun lectures and class work.

First Fridays meant that the entire school of students would assemble in line even while still in their classrooms. Each nun or lay teacher would usher her students into the hallway in double file, at a specific time. Somehow, the nuns synchronized their watches like bank robbers when it came to arranging their students in the hallway.

As we marched through the school on our way up the hill to the church, the nuns would keep the eyes in back of her head peeled for any tomfoolery going on. Nary a day passed when some kid didn't get belted for an indiscretion while in line. The nuns felt most vulnerable when their kids where loose and outside the confines of their classrooms. So they made each trip to the church seem like a march to Bataan.

Once we reached the cafeteria hallway, we had to walk outside, regardless of the weather, and take the sidewalk the final 200 yards to the church. The slope of Pleasant Avenue was pretty steep, and rather treacherous in the wintertime if Mr. Ciancetti or Joe McCrarren hadn't shoveled or salted the sidewalk.

If you were on your bike heading down the road, you could reach 40 miles an hour without pedaling for a two-minute stretch. You couldn't ride your bike up the hill unless you were a world-class cyclist trained in the French Alps.

Since it was somewhat of a trek in the cold weather, the nuns would put the class line on autopilot once we hit the outdoors. We knew we were under close surveillance by the nuns from the windows inside, so we usually stayed in line in silence. Except one day—one remarkable day following a February First Friday Mass—when the Immaculate Conception Seventh Grade revolted in unison.

We came out the door of the church and headed down the hill to the school, when Dan Volare and I started doing the Curly Shuffle while in line. It was a spontaneous tribute to The Three Stooges rather than a statement against Immaculate Conception. But in seconds, we realized how quickly a good idea can spread to 60 kids in a makeshift, double-file conga line after Mass.

With Tugboat watching in anger from the warmth of the school foyer, her class momba-ed its way from the church to the school—three-steps and a bump—laughing all the way.

I remember turning around from the front of the line and seeing the entire group of kids picking up on the cha-cha-like dance. It was unrehearsed, and undiscussed. Apparently, even the girls had watched at least some of the Stooges, because they were in on it, too.

When we got to the school door, the laughing along with the fancy, Caribbean footwork stopped. Tugboat was so furious and red in the face that she was apoplectic. She didn't know whom to slug since everyone was complicitous, so she shouted about our horrible fate to come when we arrived back in the classroom.

We marched back like Marines, only with smirks on our faces. For the first time since I'd been at I.C., the kids actually pulled one over on a nun. We had bonded as a class, unafraid of our pending doom. That's when I realized for the first time that Franklin Delano Roosevelt was right: the only thing we had to fear, was fear itself.

By the time we got to the classroom, and settled into our seats, Tugboat had blown a gasket. She must have worked herself up into a tizzy, or something, because we could tell that she had changed mentally. I think she might have been on the edge of a mental breakdown all along, just waiting for somebody or something to give her a little nudge. Something snapped in the old broad's head on the walk back to the classroom.

She began crying in the class, to the amazement of us all. I had never seen any type of human emotion emanating from a nun before; certainly never a weak human emotion like crying.

Old Tugboat was taking our little mamba down the sidewalk personally, as if we were trying to ruin her, or something.

Naturally, Tugboat had never seen the Stooges perform this little antic. She had no idea what we were doing, or how we all managed to perform this downhill dance with the perfect synchronization of the June Taylor dancers.

So she freaked out. Tugboat started sweating, then put her head down on her desk and wept, as our class, befuddled, looked around at each other as if to say, "The old broad cracked!"

The next day, Tugboat was nowhere to be found. A substitute lay teacher arrived on the scene. The stand-in teacher simply said that Sister Daniel Marie had a slight mental breakdown and needed a rest for a while.

FIRST HOLY CONUNDRUM— WHAT TO CONFESS?

Some days, the nuns would carve out a time during school for kids to go to Confession. This was usually allowed just prior to First Friday Mass, when the whole school would attend church. The premise was, get the kids to Confession so every kid in every pew has his ass up to the rail to receive Holy Communion.

A Catholic cannot receive Holy Communion during Mass unless he or she is free of sin. Coming fresh out of Confession was a good way to ensure that there was perfect attendance at the communion rail.

It was mighty embarrassing sitting back in the pew—an obvious sinner—and letting a dozen kids climb over you on their way to Communion. The nuns had you so introspective about your guilt, that you could be afraid of receiving Communion over nothing at all. If my mother asked me to water the plants before I went out to play and I didn't, was that a sin? Had I disobeyed my mother? Was it a sin? Did I break one of Moses' hand-carried covenants, "Honor thy Mother and thy Father?"

No kid filled with guilt and carrying a sinful soul to the altar's rail wanted to choke on the Host—the Body of Christ, for God's sake—in front of the entire school.

Taking Communion without a clean slate was way too risky for me. My philosophy, thanks to the nuns' indoctrination, was when in doubt, sit it out. At least people seeing me staying seated at Communion time would think I was an honest sinner, anyhow.

Somehow, the nuns embedded in our noggins that Confession was good for the soul. So I went like every other kid. We spilled our guts out to Murphy or Garbin or whoever else was available to hear our tales of deviousness.

A Catholic kid learns of his sinful ways in the Second Grade. At the tender age of seven, you're prepared to take your First Holy Communion.

This is a celebrated step in a kid's life. Why? I have no idea.

The previous six years of his life, a child has been a pain in the ass to the congregation at Mass. Crying during the gospel, fidgeting in the pew during the sermon, looking face-to-face at the people kneeling in the pew behind, dorking around in the aisle...

When the Second Grade comes along, however, it's time to become a participating part of the religion.

Your parents buy you your first suit if you're a boy. A girl gets a fancy, new dress. Somebody buys you a prayer book, and you're on your way to becoming part of the Roman Catholic club.

There is one caveat, however—that little problem of receiving Communion with sin in your heart. As important as it is to start a kid off with his First Holy Communion, no kid is sucking down the Body of Christ without having gone to Confession first. Seven years old notwithstanding.

The nuns figure that, by seven years old, you're about ripe for the world of sin. After all, you're a monosyllabic reader now for some six months. By seven years old, a kid is capable of all kinds of sin, they figure. So, before the First Holy Communion celebration, to which a kid's entire family tree will be invited, he first must be initiated with his first Confession.

I remember my first Confession. It was the first time I can remember sinning. Sister Rose Timothy explained the set up to the entire second grade.

First, you kneel in a pew and watch the two doors in the corner of the church. Those were the confessionals. They were like little dark closets. It was spooky then and it's still spooky even as an adult. You walk up this meshed, speakeasy-type cabinet and kneel down on its built-in kneeler. The priest on the other side of the wall has a little sliding window that shows his silhouette, and allows you to confess your wayward ways without having to look him in the eyeball. Since he's supposed to be God's liaison in this matter, we were told not to hold back. Feel comfortable telling him everything and anything on your mind.

So, you wait for the little red light to go off above the doorway of the Confessional, and this signals that the room is free for the next sinner. It's kind of like the "occupado" sign on the bathroom of an airplane. You couldn't help but think about the sins the guy in front of you was bestowing on the priest, especially if he was in there for more than five minutes.

You could watch a pious, old woman go into Confession, knowing she was deeply religious, and an honorable citizen. But if she stayed in that box more than 10 minutes, you were sure she was Lizzy Borden when she came out.

While waiting my turn, I rehearsed what I was going to say. The nuns taught that you didn't go in the Confessional and dilly-dally. I always saw it as a shit-and-git experience. I had it all down pat and ready to rip. The sooner I spilled the beans, the faster I'd be out of there, and the less likely waiting confessors wouldn't think I was involved in the Lindbergh baby kidnapping.

The biggest problem with First Holy Communion is, what the hell to confess. At seven years old, you can hardly reach the door handle of the Confessional, for chrissake. There really should be a mark on the door like at amusement parks that prohibits kids too small from entering.

Nevertheless, I remember walking inside and noticing the confessional was like a little, haunted house. I knelt down and the priest slid open his door and whispered to me through the translucent mesh. At least we were whispering, I thought. I could tell by his silhouette that it was Father Carsello, a great guy who left Immaculate Conception the following year.

So I whispered back my refrain that I was taught:

"Bless me, Father, for I have sinned. This is my first confession."

At subsequent confessions, you were expected to state how long it has been since your last confession. The priest likes to get a time frame on your sinning habits.

"Okay, my son, what are your sins?" the priest asked.

"I disobeyed my mother and father three times, I told a lie twice and I stole something once."

(This admittance was my standard confession for years to come. It was simple and direct. Nothing flashy, but enough to show that I'm a contrite sinner. At seven years old, I hadn't mastered the skills of sarcasm, e.g. admitting to three counts of adultery, two counts of coveting my neighbor's goods, and one instance of murder.)

Then Carsello gave me his blessing, and sent me out of the dark with my assignment: 10 Hail Marys and 10 Our Fathers as my penance. No big deal. I made up some sins, blabbed them out, and paid the price for it with a handful of prayers.

When I came out the room, another first-timer went in. I get it, I thought. It's a revolving door of soul cleansing. I then went to the rail, buried my head in my hands, and silently rattled off my penance.

Before long, I was on my way, relieved. Finally, after seven sinful years of infancy and early childhood, I was free from sin. I could feel the burden lifted off my back. The expunging of seven sinful years was like dropping a piano off my shoulders. At last I had a clean slate, and I was heading back into the world of temptation and mayhem with a clear conscience. Now God and the nuns would be satisfied that my seven-year-old soul was clean enough to take on the Sacrament of Holy Communion. Hallelujah!

LYING IN THE CONFESSIONAL

One time, when I was ten years old, I entered a confessional and was greeted by an unfamiliar priest. I immediately realized that this confession wasn't going to be a perfunctory shit-and-git to which I had been accustomed.

I crowed out my usual sins: "Disobeyed my parents three times, lied twice and stole something once."

Then this mystery priest does the unthinkable. He wants to discuss these discretions.

"Why did you disobey your parents?" he asked.

"Why?" I questioned, not so much his query, but his reason for asking.

"Why did you disobey?" he insisted.

"I—-don't know. Whatta ya mean?" I said, stalling for a chance to think of some way I disobeyed.

"You know it's wrong to disobey your parents," he elaborated. "Your mother and father work hard every day to put food on your table and to send you to a fine school where...blah-bl-blah..."

I needed a quick disobedience to spill out for this nosey priest. I thought of one! One time, my mother wouldn't allow me to watch a hockey game on TV after getting an underwhelming grade on a test in fourth grade. Not allowing hockey games was the perfect, parental punishment for me. Depriving me from watching Bobby Hull and the Chicago Blackhawks was tantamount to tying me to a rack. So, I used it as a premise for being disobedient.

"I watched a hockey game when I was told not to," I lied, hoping this fabrication would satisfy his inquiry.

The priest rebutted, "If your mother tells you not to watch TV, you have to understand that she's doing it for your own good. There's such a thing as right and wrong, and you're going to have to learn the difference. Your mother's job is to... blah-bl-blah, blah blah."

I was sweating just listening to him reading me the riot act from the cheap seat of his confessional. Jesus Christ! Give me a break, will ya?

When the priest finally finished his diatribe about how the world would be a better place without disobedient kids like me, I readied myself for the longest penance ever. Instead, he asks me another question.

"What did you steal?"

"What?" I didn't know what he was talking about.

"You said you stole something. What was it?" he asked, interested as hell in my sinful life.

I started to get a fever. A rush of heat ran all through me. I realized that I was about to drop my second lie in five minutes on this inquisitive priest.

My mind searched for something to steal. What could it be? Not candy at the store, that's a crime. I'm not doing that penance. Money from my mother's purse? No. This guy will make me repay it to my mother, and she already trusts me with her purse. If I pay her 25 cents for stealing, she may never trust me again. Besides, where would I get the 25 cents? I'd have to steal it from my mother to repay her for something I never stole in the first place! This priest was turning me into John Dillinger, for chrissake!

I answered the priest by trying to be vague.

"Ah, it was something little, nothing important," I said, attempting to shake his attention with the venality of it all.

"Well, certainly it was something important enough to make you confess it. What did you steal?" he persisted.

I began to panic. Son-of-a-bitch, I thought, what is this, Judgment Day? The goddam Spanish Inquisition, for Christ aloud? I gotta think of something, fast! Come-on, I said to myself, think! Think, you pretend kleptomaniac, you!

At that point, a unique scenario dashed through my head. If I bolt out of here right now, I figured, I can leave this inquisitive priest in the dark. I'll run through the church and slip into a crowd, and he'll never catch me.

I never heard of anyone ever running out of a confessional before. There's probably not even a sin labeled to that kind of exit. After all, I thought, how many guys are in Hell right now because they bolted out of a confessional in mid-confession?

My imaginary version of The Great Escape died quickly in my head as I envisioned Sister Agnes Marita or some other nun probably lurking right outside the confessional like a security guard waiting to leap onto any confessional escapers.

At last, my conscience came to the rescue. I thought about an incident that happened two years ago at my neighbor's house. I figured I could parlay that recollection into a lie.

The truth went like this. My nine-year-old friend, Sandy Scanton, had a little sale of toys and crap in her basement, and I saw a little, fuzzy bear about the size of a cigarette lighter that I liked. When I forked over the quarter for it, Sandy told me she couldn't sell it to me because little Donna Nester had run home to get 25 cents from her mother to buy it.

I carried on like an Arab camel trader, convincing Sandy that Donna wasn't coming back. Besides, money talks. One couldn't walk into a candy store and say, "Hey, Mack, hold that taffy apple for me until I get back with my money, okay?" I threw all the devious logic I could at the confused girl until she sold the little bear to me, out of exhaustion.

I took it and went home. And I always wondered about the emptiness and despair little Donna Nester felt when she learned that I bought this little bear that she cherished, right out from under her nose.

It was such a selfish act on my part that I figured I could re-configure this incident into a full-fledged lie to satisfy this persnickety priest.

I told him the story about the bear, only adding that I stole it from Sandy instead of paying the quarter as I really did.

"Well, son, I trust you know the right thing to do," he acknowledged.

"Yes, Father."

"What are you going to do?" he questioned.

"Uh, I'm going to pray for God's forgiveness?" I asked, hoping this was his reasoning, too.

"Well, yes, that too. But certainly you must return this little bear to its rightful owner. After all, you stole it, and it doesn't belong to you. You need to do the right thing, my son."

"Return it?" I asked, thinking about how in the world that would be possible.

I threw that stupid little bear in the garbage can two days after I bought it. It was for sissies, anyhow. Or, at least for little girls like Donna Nester. Now this guy wants me to return this thing to a girl who I bought it from two years ago. That little bear is buried 30 feet in the city dump by now.

I just kept getting deeper and deeper into my own bullshit.

"Yes, Father, I'll return the little bear," I said in despair, realizing that in fifteen minutes of confession with this priest I had just lied three times. All I needed now was for a cock to crow somewhere in the church, signaling the new Judas among the crowd.

Finally, the priest had had enough of me and he dished out his penance. While I braced myself, expecting to receive life without parole, he gives me a paltry three Hail Marys and an Act of Contrition.

I couldn't believe my ears! That's like getting a free pass out of jail. My soul was cleansed, and my penance a mere bag of shells. I was delighted. I left the confessional a new kid, invigorated and encouraged by my newfound sinlessness.

That is, until I opened the door and looked at the faces waiting to use my confessional. They looked at me suspiciously, as if I had sold nuclear secrets to the Russians. I guess I had exceeded that five-minute grace period in the confessional, when one gradually goes from Francis of Assisi to Jack the Ripper with every tick of the clock.

ALTAR BOY— FROM LATIN TO PIG-LATIN

The sixth grade was a precipitous point in a boy's life in Catholic School. At Immaculate Conception, it was the year a boy could become an altar boy.

One day, Sister Mary Olive, the nun who handled the choir and music arrangements for the church, appeared in our classroom. Without allowing her audience a chance for much thought, she asked for a show of hands of the boys who were interested in becoming altar boys.

My father had been an altar boy, and so was my brother. It seemed obvious that I'd be one. I thrust my hand up first. The nun counted the hands of about half the boys in the class then explained the duties of her newly volunteered altar boys.

First, she said, an altar boy's behavior is impeccable. Second, he's never late, never missing a Mass to which he's been assigned. Third, he must learn his prayers at the steps of the altar and the altar boys' responses throughout the Mass—in Latin! And, he had to learn all the functions of the altar boys during both high and low Masses, whether he be a candle bearer or a cross bearer.

It was a daunting task, but being a part of the Mass was something that seemed to bestow great honor on a boy. Besides, maybe the nuns would back off a bit on a guy who chose to assist in the functions of the Mass, I thought. Perhaps, I reasoned, altar boys would receive favored status around the school. There could be privileges and special treatment that went along with being an altar boy. I figured the nuns would, at least, give a wink and a nod to borderline grades. Certainly in Christian Doctrine...Wrong again, wolf breath!

I soon learned that being an altar boy was no bargaining chip to a nun. To them, what you did on your own time, was of no consequence. They figured that boys naturally became altar boys for the shear fun of it. After all, who wouldn't want to serve 6:15 a.m. Mass before school in the wintertime?

Learning the Latin was tough, but I dove in like everything else: I made a contest out of it. My goal was to be the first of all the would-be altar boys to learn his Latin. In three days, I had learned each of the seven prayers, including the lengthy Confiteor, which was the second-longest thing I'd ever memorized, after "Casey at the Bat."

I was the second kid to learn his Latin completely. John Lorrenzo had the same idea of being first, only he actually accomplished it.

The measure of knowing one's Latin really well was based on two factors: 1) how close you came phonetically to the actual Latin words, and 2) how fast you could rattle your prayers off.

Normally in Catholic School, diction would be important along with projection and eye contact. Well, none of that was important being an altar boy. At least not at I.C.

The most important trait of an altar boy serving with the curmudgeon Monsignor Murphy was to say your prayers faster than a Southern auctioneer. God help you if you couldn't talk faster than Evelyn Wood could read. God forbid if you got stage fright and forgot your prayers at the foot of the altar. Murf would be on you like stink on a camel.

One morning, I was the sole altar boy serving 8 a.m. Mass with Murf. While still in the sacristy, before Mass, Murf was bitching. He wanted to start early, for some reason. Basically because he was a bastard, I guess.

I hurried to get dressed. I went to the closet where all sizes of the long, black cassocks and white blouse surpluses were kept.

It was always difficult to find my size. I was about the smallest size, and there were several cassocks that fit, but I learned to look at the sleeves first before choosing one for Mass. There were many cassocks that had dried snot on the sleeves, and I was always careful to avoid those. Nothing was worse than holding your hands to prayer for an hour and having to look at some altar boy's snot caked on your sleeve.

(It wasn't until my final year of being an altar boy that I learned those dried cakey spots on the sleeve wasn't altar boy snot at all. It was wax drippings from the candles that we carried.)

Murf started screaming.

"It's not a low Mass, it's a high Mass!" he hollered, meaning I had to light four more candles on the altar.

I grabbed the long, brass candle apparatus that had an extendible wick on one side and a flame-snuffing cup on the other. I lit the wick on one of the already lighted candles and attempted to light the other four candles on the altar.

As the churchgoers found their pews and watched my candle lighting, I struggled to transfer fire to each candle, which were barely within my reach. With arms overhead, I finally got all but one candle lit, but the fourth candle just wouldn't take a torch.

Unable to pry up the wick of the candle from my position without using the altar as a scaffold, I had to hope for divine intervention to get the reluctant candle to light. Over my shoulder, I could see Murf gesturing, and grumbling "Come on, come on."

At last, saving me from turning to salt right before the altar, a man from the congregation came forward, reached high up to the candle and adjusted the flattened wick. He then lit it for me with a match. I scurried back to the sacristy to get my candle that I'd carry onto the altar with the grumpy bastard by my side.

Murf was draped with his priest robe while I was adorned in my long, black, front-buttoned cassock and white surplus that bloused over. I carried the candle nice and straight while Murf brought the Good Book with him.

I put down my candle and knelt at the steps of the altar and prepared for the priest and altar boy's volley of Latin prayers. I bowed my head and machine-gunned out my Latin:

"Ad Deum qui laetificat juventutem meam. "

Murf grumbled while I recited my prayers, impatient as an old man in a dress shop.

"Come on, come on…" grouched the petulant priest.

I went as fast as I could.

"Misereatur tui omnipotens Deus, et dimissis peccatis tuis, perducat te ad vitam aeternam."

"Come on, come on!" groused the sour puss.

Finally, I just said the Confiteor prayer in pure jibberish, about twice the speed of sound. I sounded like an Indian doing a rain dance chant.

"Ahhahh-yaa-aaah-hhiihhh, haommmonnni-yaha, yacka-ma-hay-ya."

After that ridiculous rendition of prayers I realized how ludicrous a Latin Mass really was.

We could have done the whole Mass in pig-Latin and nobody would have known the difference.

Each Sunday in the church bulletin, the new week's schedule of altar boy assignments was posted. If your name was on the list for the week, you were presented with the good news and the bad news.

If you got 6:15 a.m. Mass, Monday thru Wednesday, the bad news was the time in the morning you had to serve. I had to get up by 5 a.m., and ride my bicycle to church lugging my schoolbooks. This was particularly difficult since a) my bicycle sucked (I was constantly dragging a fender) and b) the book bag hadn't been invented yet. The bicycle ride was a one-handed balancing act trying to keep the two-wheeler upright and my books and lunch bag under my arm. It also meant I had to ride my bike home from school instead of taking the bus.

The good news about 6:15 a.m. Mass was that you served for Father Garbin instead of the cantankerous Monsignor Murphy. Garbin was easy to serve for. He didn't expect the altar boys to say their prayers at 78 rpm, and he wasn't a bastard.

The biggest difference between the old codger and the corpulent one when serving Mass was the amount of wine they consumed. One altar boy brings to the altar the wine and water in cruets similar to oil and vinegar salad bottles. The other altar boy brings a dish and a towelette the size of a handkerchief.

The priest holds his fingers together over his gold chalice while the altar boy pours wine into the cup and then the water over his fingers. The priest then wipes his hands on the towelette, folds it, and hands it back to the altar boy.

Garbin loved his wine albeit 6:15 in the morning. I emptied many a wine cruet into his gold chalice. He sure didn't like the water, though. My pouring water into the cup was only symbolic when Garbin was celebrating Mass. If you attempted to put even a drop into his chalice, he'd raise the cup high and away, as if the water were hemlock.

Murphy didn't like much wine. He was a teatotaler compared to Garbin. Murphy would take about a thimble of wine and a shot of water. He'd dry off his hands and just fling the towelette at the altar boy. His manners would have made Emily Post slap the crap out of him.

While Murphy was bitching all the time at something, I only saw Garbin yell one time at us altar boys. And we deserved it. Scott Witner, Dan Volare and I were serving a funeral one time during school hours. Somehow, we all caught the giggles, a contagious affliction that is extremely hard to exorcise, especially while serving a funeral Mass during school time.

Horribly stupid jokes became hysterical when you're immature and getting out of school for an hour. While the casket was brought in, we were asking each other who the guy was in the refrigerator. We made fun of a goofy looking mourner, and horsed around during the funeral proceedings. We did little imperceptible things to a mourning audience, like cross eyes at each other, or cut farts while kneeling along the altar.

Garbin had had enough when Witner bumped Volare's arm as he was preparing to ring the bells at Eucharist time. The pre-mature jingle of the bells and our laughing set him off. He came over to us and whispered a warning to us, which pretty much wiped the grins off our smirking faces. The rotund priest gave us what's for when the funeral Mass was over. Fortunately, Garbin didn't go ratting on us to Sister Mary Olive, the nun in charge of altar boys, and the sole executioner.

One early morning, Ray Dempster and I served 6:15 a.m. Mass together in the gym, which was temporarily converted into the church. We both got there so early, that Garbin hadn't been in yet to turn on the lights.

As we looked out from the stage area into the darkened, pewed rows, we could see it was silent and still. So Dempster had the brainstorm to turn on the old gym scoreboard, just for the fun of it. With nobody around, it seemed like an innocuous sort of church prank. So we cranked the scoreboard up. To our amazement, the huge scoreboard high on the wall blasted out a basketball buzzer sound repeatedly while flashing white and red lights. The thing came alive like a roaring robot, lighting the whole church with its flashing bulbs and shattering the silence with its timeout buzzers.

Between the shadows of the flashing lights, to our horror, we saw five or six parishioners kneeling in various pews. We immediately turned off the scoreboard and questioned each other on our possible fate. If someone tells Sister Mary Olive that we set the scoreboard off prior to Mass, she would have a conniption unlike anything ever seen before. Was this grounds for dismissal from altar boys? Absolutely. No question. Maybe it even justified a school assembly to showcase our tar and feathering. We held our breath for the next three hours until class started. Somehow, nobody told on us, and no nun trouble befell us. I guess the novenas we were saying for our lives to be spared got us through that morning.

About the worst job you could have as an I.C. altar boy was to assist Murf when he did the Stations of the Cross. The old coot performed this 14-step process of Jesus' last days with all the energy of a noodle.

He would kneel and read from his book while propping his head with one hand as if he had a toothache during the whole ordeal.

"Jeee-zzzuzzz falls for the third time, Our Father, who art in heaven..." he'd growl with his hand muffling his voice. You just wanted to hit him in the face with a mooshy tomato.

Even with the entire school in attendance, Murf couldn't muster enough enthusiasm to make one feel he gave a shit about what he was doing. It really was the nuns that kept the religious teaching and the spirit of Catholicism going at I.C. Monsignor Murphy should have been given his walking papers, in my opinion. He didn't seem to understand what his role was as a priest, to say nothing about being monsignor. He acted more like a prisoner of his own church.

THE CHARACTER ASSASSINATION OF FELICIA

I'm pretty sure it wasn't easy being a girl at Immaculate Conception. They seemed to be in as much torture as the boys. They got slapped around on occasion, too, and were the targets of the nuns' ire almost as much as the boys. The girls just weren't as bad as the boys.

In hindsight, my grade class throughout the years boasted some very attractive girls. The only trouble is, a pretty girl seemed to walk more in the crosshairs of a nun than a non-pretty girl.

The nuns could remove a girl's attractiveness by drawing attention to her frailties.

One time, Sister Michael Ann descended on Mary Galloway for not knowing her place during reading class. The nun humiliated the girl infront of the class, then grilled her with questions that nobody in the class could answer. In 60 seconds, a nun could make a girl look stupid, then leave her hang out to dry for the rest of the year as some worthless dumb-shit.

Sister Veronica once caught Kim Davis daydreaming during Civics class. The nun pounced on the unsuspecting girl like a quiz show host.

"Maybe Kim would like to explain to the class what foreign aid is," the nun suggested.

Kim snapped to attention after hearing her name and asked the nun to repeat the question.

"What's foreign aid?" the nun reiterated.

Confidently, Kim replied, "Twelve!"

The class erupted with laughter as the doubting girl double-checked her math on her fingers.

Grinning at the pleasure of her embarrassing the girl, the victorious nun asked sarcastically, "Are you sure, Kim?"

The girl, after hearing the guffaws of her classmates began doubting even her own counting.

"I think so," she replied.

"Well, young lady," the nun proclaimed condescendingly, "maybe if you paid attention once in a while, you would know this isn't math class; it's civics."

A nun's determined scrutiny and chiding could snuff a girl's attractiveness away like an old cigar butt. In grade school, some girls seemed outright stupid with the nuns riding their backs. Later in life, throughout high school and college, I discovered those same girls weren't stupid at all. They were victims of intimidation and scorn by the nuns.

Sometimes a girl could never get out from under her own shadow at Immaculate Conception. They certainly were typecast from year to year.

The most vicious and senseless attack on a girl was served up by the irrepressible Mrs. Sezzo. This cruel misogynist once called on Felicia Pycheski, a new kid to the school, who had the misfortune to be initiated to Immaculate Conception while in Sezzo's third-grade class. After about one month, Felicia was settling in to her new surroundings and getting to know a few girls. She was quiet and unsure of herself, as any kid would be coming into I.C., not to mention landing in Sezzo's lair.

The wire-haired, old bitty called on Felicia to recite the next paragraph in our text, when out of the blue the witch asked, "Ah, Felicia? Your last name—Pycheski—is that Polish?"

The entire class of third-graders trained their eyes and ears on Felicia for her answer. When the new student answered affirmatively, a collective sigh spread through the room.

Sezzo had the answer she wanted. She had just successfully painted another student with humiliation. In 1962, Polish jokes were at its zenith. To a third grader at that time, being Polish was akin to having B.O.

The ridicule of Felicia being a "Polock" swept through the school. From that point on, thanks to Sezzo's insensitive perspicacity, this innocent girl with the long, blonde, braided hair, became a tainted and tormented person.

The most popular game on the playground became a game of tag that transmitted the imaginary disease, "Pycheski." Kids would chase each other around, day after day, tagging each other while proclaiming "You've got Pycheski!" The tagged kid receiving the Polish disease would squeal in horror until passing it on to another kid.

Felicia Pycheski was a victim of character assassination. And her assassin was the diabolical Mrs. Sezzo.

Never did a teacher, nun or priest, let alone Mrs. Sezzo, stand up and put an end to this poor kid's suffering. It was impossible for anyone to not know how pernicious this ridicule was on a kid among her peers. Why, a nun can spot a kid chewing gum in a tree two miles away, or hear a whisper in a crowded hallway. Surely, they could hear the Polock trash talk.

In fifteen minutes, a good teacher could have given a history lesson of Poland to the class, and turned Felicia Pycheski from a pariah into a prima donna. A two-minute story of courageous Polish citizens defying Hitler, or the nation's heroic soldiers on horseback charging Nazi tanks would have sent Felicia to the pantheon of pupils.

But no help came from the Immaculate Conception faculty. The psychological damage that Felicia suffered daily must have been unbearable.

As the months wore on, I noticed some girls bravely befriending Felicia. Somehow, the new girl with Polish ancestry was able to keep her head up and maintain her dignity through the most vile ridicule I've ever witnessed.

I never saw Felicia confront anyone about it. She never complained. She never cried. She never stopped attending classes or participating in events. Yet, I don't remember her smiling much. I know I couldn't have taken the misery that was bestowed upon her every day. I would have had to hop a boxcar to get out of town, or join the circus. She was without doubt the bravest kid I ever knew. The only way she could be paid back for her lost childhood is to win the lottery. A $10 million prize, that'd just about cover the damage, I'd say.

THE BALLOON

Even being a near genius and an angelic kid wasn't enough slack for Ellen Mallory.

One day, the class' smartest kid brought a project to school that utilized two pink balloons.

Naturally, the project was beautiful, and Ellen got her usual "A." But for all her intellect, she didn't anticipate the deviousness of her fellow students.

As the class lined up along the chalkboard to exit the room after school, Ellen held her project and talked to Sister Daniel Marie about her efforts. Standing behind Ellen waiting to leave were Mike Womsley and me. Eyeing the big, plump balloons, Womsley mimed to me that he was going to pop Ellen's balloon. I grinned in disbelief, knowing that such a despicable act surely would be grounds for strict punishment.

Taking the tacit dare, Womsley removed a pin from the bulletin board, and with a sheepish grimace toward me, moved the pin into position.

I watched his hand incredulously as the pin neared its target. I shook my head rapidly while laughing, hoping to call off his impending prick. Suddenly, the balloon exploded like it was filled with gunpowder. Tugboat nearly jumped out of her cowl with fright. Half the kids in the room screamed.

I continued to watch Womsley casually drop the pin like a hit man drops a .38 special. He then turns into Laurence Olivier doing a nonchalance that would have made Stanislavski proud. His performance was worthy of an academy award.

Tugboat must have soiled her shorts. I never saw her so pissed off. She grabbed Ellen Mallory by one of her pigtails and angrily pulled her head around and around, screaming "What's the matter with you? Can't you be careful?"

All the innocent Ellen Mallory could do while having her neck wrenched by Tugboat was utter repeatedly, "I don't know what happened?"

In the meantime, the bell rang and the class dismissed, while Tugboat continued to twirl Ellen's head around like a lasso.

LET THE
BEATINGS BEGIN

Every kid had to be careful of the snitchers. Even your best friend could turn on you at the pressure of a nun.

In fifth grade, Ed Dilliard fingered Ray Gracie for writing a note at his desk. The tattletale inexplicably raised his hand and announced to Sister Agnes Marita that Ray was writing something.

Gracie looked around, astonished that he'd been noticed and now called upon.

"Bring whatever your writing up here, Raymond," demanded the tall nun.

Gracie started to stuff the note in his pocket when the nun spoke again.

"Don't put it away. Bring it up here."

Gracie shuffled his feet all the way up to the front of the classroom and handed over the note.

The nun read it, frowned, then demanded that he write his note on the board ten times for the rest of the class to see what he was writing.

Crimson with embarrassment, Gracie started writing on the chalkboard in hieroglyphics. Sister Agnes Marita made him erase his "chicken scratch" and write legibly.

So Gracie started writing legibly, but so small that even a diamond cutter's magnifying glass couldn't reveal the words.

Sister chastised him again for his writing and demanded that he write larger.

Then Gracie decided to write his sentences underneath the hanging papers above the chalkboard.

Finally, disguising his sentences were no use. He got on to writing what was on his note. It read, "Dear stupid sister, I think you are a dope."

In seventh grade, Mike Camden and I had devised a brilliant method for passing notes to each other, until Mike Banyon turned double agent.

We both sat by the chalkboard along the side row, he a few seats ahead of me. We'd write a note, pin it to the chalk eraser, and slide the eraser back and forth along the chalk tray like a monorail conveyance.

It was a beautiful innovation, quiet and efficient, until Banyon blew the whistle.

He stood up and announced that Mike was passing notes. Somehow I wasn't implicated, but I waited nervously for the other shoe to drop.

Sister Michael Ann was a quick judge and jury. Without asking any questions, she immediately made Camden move his desk up to the front of the class, turn the desk around, and face the class for the rest of the day. Fortunately for me, Sister didn't ask who was on the other end of the notes.

Don Mintori once ratted on himself and a group of his friends who threw eggs at the school during Halloween. To the disbelief of the others, Mintori told Sister Alphonsa Marie voluntarily how he, Marco, Volare and Kevin had given the school an egg shampoo.

Somehow, a kid could feel rewarded for telling the truth even if it sent himself and his friends to the guillotine.

Each nun had her own style of punishment to fit any crime.

Sister Ann Bernadette went bonkers with anger toward me once in seventh grade. I enjoyed tapping the metal sides of my desk with my fingers, imitating the sound of a running horse's hooves. Until the nun had had enough. She called me up to the front of the room, grabbed her three-sided ruler, and told me to extend my hand.

I remember looking back at the class and smiling a second before the nun began playing a drum role on my knuckles with her ruler. Her face furled with anger as she whacked the horse sense out of my fingers. For all the pounding she did on my knuckles, I was surprised that the chopping didn't hurt much, considering her ruler was about as heavy as a nunchuku.

The worst clobbering I ever got came at the hands of the indomitable Mrs. Sezzo in third grade.

The old hag had just given an order while turning around toward the board. Apparently, I was the only one who didn't hear her mumbled demand, since every desktop went up but mine.

I then opened my desk lid like everyone else, then turned my head to my neighbor to ask what the hell Sezzo had said. Before I could get the answer, the old bitch noticed my talking, walked down to my desk, lifted the lid up further from my head, then bashed the lid down on my skull.

"That will teach you from talking to your neighbor," Sezzo triumphantly proclaimed as she waddled back to the front of the class. I sniffled with a bump on my head for the next two hours.

Mrs. McCaffery, another slaphappy lay teacher with a penchant for innovative punishment was clever about her lickings.

She used to keep by her desk a thick, wooden paddle the shape of a two-foot-long 2x4 with a little handle on it. Inscribed across it was "Board of Education." Whenever a kid got out of line, she's ask them if they wanted to be introduced to her Board of Education.

When McCaffery did decide to use her Board of Education, the punishment looked like something out of a Sigma Chi hazing. A kid would be told to bend over and hold his knees, and McCaffery would give him a whack that would spin his eyes around.

She once threw her leather key case at Landry in the second row because he wasn't paying attention. When her house and car keys crashed on his desk, he woke up, startled.

McCaffery was a black belt at hand-to-hand combat. She pulled Tom King completely out of his seat and to the front of the room by his earlobe.

She loved the behind the head crack, which always set a kid's head flying comically forward with a slapping sound.

McCaffery knew she could pound big kids like David Pasqualoni, Jeff Ralston and Chris Keshawn to her heart's content. McCaffery knew how to slap them so hard on the back that their chest cavities echoed the blow.

Sister Alphonsa Marie was a finger pointer and a chin grabber. She'd waggle her arthritic index finger in your face if you weren't completely tuned in to her class.

One day, Bob Carlton lost his place in history, so Sister Alphonsa Marie took a hold of his chin with one hand and tossed the pages in his text to the correct spot with the other. For half the day, he wore her finger marks on his jaw.

Both the teachers and the students could be gross at times. Kids—boys particularly—are gross by nature, but teachers aren't always debutantes.

Mrs. Sezzo stopped her class right in its tracks to shout out to a busy student, "Tazmilio stop picking your nose! You wanna suck on my feet!"

At the time, I couldn't decide which I wanted to throw up from, the sight of Tazmilio digging for treasure or the vision of him sucking on Sezzo's smelly, open-toe shoe. How Sezzo equated sucking on her feet as a substitute for nosepicking was beyond my comprehension.

Ed Dilliard always had an earful of orange wax. John Sarducci sneezed into his hands then wiped the mess all over his pants. Ron Tazmilio's teeth were as yellow as corn. Chris Keshawn had an agonizingly harsh cough, that sounded like he had tuberculosis. Donna DeSoto had gigantic boobs and a mustache ever since the fourth grade. Kids were cutting farts loose constantly in class. Even a nun didn't have a comeback for those. They pretty much let the flatulence go unchallenged.

Tazmilio was a notorious farter, and he wasn't even ashamed of it. He felt that any kind of attention was a good thing. It wasn't hard to understand, either, in his case. He came from a family of eight kids. He wasn't the best looking kid in our class, but he was still a head turner. When he rang one out, everybody turned around to see him smirking proudly.

Nobody else in class dared steal Tazmilio's spotlight for farting. Being recognized for farting was indeed a dubious distinction. After nine years, virtually every kid has slid one out, even if by accident. The trick was to remain anonymous as the incriminating evidence wafted through the air.

One time, I was holding back my bladder so hard in class that I accidentally forced out an audible gaser. Twenty kids turned their heads toward me, grimacing with grossed-out looks on their faces. In an instant of genius, I whirled in my own seat and groaned at Joe Landry sitting behind me.

Landry was the perfect fall guy. He wasn't even paying attention, so when he looked up to see everyone staring at him, he grinned stupidly. His guilt was sealed, and he didn't even know what was going on.

Another time, I heard Richard Coffet rip one right next to me. Mary Crambles heard the fart and surely felt the vibration of the blast, as I did. In disgust, she turned around and gave Coffet a dirty look. Coffet, blushing, decided to act like he had faked the fart intentionally by blowing into his arm. The feeble audition didn't even sound the same, and the girl didn't buy it.

The nuns didn't show great laundry habits with, well, their habits. The nuns figured that since they wore the same bloody thing every day that nobody would be any the wiser as to how often they changed clothes, if at all. But a nun's undoing was the classroom chalkboard. Since the chalkboard and the chalk tray were always right behind the nun's desk, she would be in possible contact with it virtually all day long.

If a nun wasn't careful when conducting class, she could back into the chalkboard and leave a reverse imprint of the lesson on her black veil.

Sister Veronica once carried a math equation on her veil for a week. I guess fellow nuns don't help out each other with telltale chalk marks.

Knowing the insidious damage chalk could do to a nun, kids would grind little chalk granules onto Sister's chair for her to sit on. It wasn't unusual to see nuns walking up and down the aisles with a crummy, white-specked butt. It kind of made us feel like we had something to say in response to all the humiliation and torture that the nuns directed at us. It was our little touche back at the nuns.

Nuns would have made great Mohels.

PHYSICAL EDUCATION— CATHOLIC STYLE

Although Immaculate Conception had one of the best gymnasiums in the entire North Shore, it was converted into a makeshift church for much of my tenure as a student. From third through sixth grade, the old school and church up on the hill was being demolished to make room for the new, contemporary church. In the meantime, the pews from the old church were screwed into the floor of the gym, removing any hope of versatility.

Schooling without a gym at Immaculate Conception suited both Monsignor Murphy and principal Sister Eileen just fine. I.C. children didn't need sports and recreation, they figured. I.C. kids could read about other kids participating in those concepts in a book.

So when it came to physical education, I.C. took a passive if not abolitionist approach. Students would have to bring their own shorts and T-shirt and tennis shoes to class and change clothes right at their desks. Naturally, the girls changed elsewhere. The nun would step out in the doorway but leave their hands on the door while kids got dressed for gym. No I.C. nun would dare completely leave the room, even while students dressed, lest someone would seize the opportunity to talk to their neighbor.

Physical education usually consisted of one day a week, for one class period's duration. That meant, by the time students dressed, lined up, walked outside to the playground and met up with the gym teacher, 25 percent of the class was over.

By the time the gym teacher took attendance, yelled at us for not lining up straight, and ran us through a Parris Island-style calisthenics program, there was about 10 minutes left to play dodge ball or softball.

We could never get more than one inning in before the bell rang for us to dismiss gym class. It almost wasn't worth the trouble. By the time we got inside, we were either sweaty or freezing, depending on the time of year. Then we got dressed at our seats again, and tried to get back to more classwork.

I remember when President Kennedy started the President's Council on Physical Fitness. Even Immaculate Conception got into the act. Suddenly, we were doing push ups and sit ups and lots of running.

But without a gym in which to play basketball or to host other physical activities, I.C. was a graveyard for up and developing athletes.

The nuns felt we had the best of all worlds: a church conveniently converted from a gym, and a new church being built at the same time. What could be better? Two churches in one!

Even when the new church finally opened and the pews were at last removed from the gym, the school administration remained satisfied with the dormancy of its recreation facilities.

There was little or no effort to offer sports to the students who had virtually never known the combination of physical and academic participation.

Then along rode into town a maverick of a nun, Sister Stephen. I don't know where she came from, but suddenly she was a part of the faculty. As any outsider would notice, there was a beautiful gymnasium sitting across from the cafeteria doing nothing.

Sister Stephen questioned why there was no Immaculate Conception basketball team, and the principal's answer came back, because there isn't one, that's why. There's no coach and no equipment, and besides, why create more work for ourselves, the administration figured. The school had gone without a useful gym for five years, why worry about it now.

The ambivalence of I.C. faculty wasn't good enough for Sister Stephen. So, the spunky nun took it upon herself to be the new Immaculate Conception basketball coach. A nun, a basketball coach...Good intention, horrible reality.

I immediately went out for the team and found myself and eight classmates lined up with Sister Stephen leading drills.

Still decked out in her normal nun wear, including black-heeled shoes, Sister Stephen blew the whistle around her neck and instructed us on basketball fundamentals. Watching this nun, complete in her piety, attempt to demonstrate a hook shot is imbedded in my mind forever. With her veil flagging and rosary beads tossing, Sister Stephen dribbled in a crouch with one hand, scooped the ball up with the other, and tossed the ball in the general direction of the rim. With every step, her shoes clapped the gym floor like a flamingo dancer. It was the single-most pathetic thing I'd ever seen at Immaculate Conception.

Undaunted, Sister Stephen persisted, and Immaculate Conception fielded a team. Our first game was at Our Lady of Perpetual Health, a wealthy school in a nearby suburb. OLPH had a real team, a real coach, and even real fans.

Immaculate Conception didn't allow us to use a bus nor did it provide any transportation. Our team had to find the facility on our own.

Not only were we embarrassed showing up on our side of the court with a nun leading the way, we took the court without uniforms.

Of all the kids on the floor, I was the most pathetic looking. I had forgotten to bring white socks with me, so I was forced to play on the court in black dress socks. For some reason, playing sockless was either illegal or un-Catholic-like. It was more important that I looked ridiculous.

Early in the game, I experienced more embarrassment when the referee called me for a foul. As he attempted to report the foul to the official scorer, he noticed I didn't even have a number on my jersey. The game had to stop while they "numbered" me zero in the official book. I guess I'd rather be zero in the book rather than "black socks."

The game was a nightmare. We got obliterated and humiliated by the rocking, stomping crowd at OLPH. The crowd heckled our coach for being a nun, and us players for being total dweebs.

The next game, we hosted neighboring St. James, a school with an athletic program nearly as extinct as ours. Sister taught us a 2-3 zone on defense, and we implemented it to perfection. St. James' coach taught his kids a box and one defense, and we stalemated each other to the depths of utter boredom.

With the score 4 to 2 at halftime, Sister encouraged us to forge a comeback. The second half was fraught with turnovers. Both teams dribbled the ball as if the court was on a 45-degree angle.

Our own home fans looked on as if they were watching a chess match. Occasionally I'd hear a frustrated fan from the stands yell encouragement like "Come on, I.C.! Let's wake up out there!"

Both zones proved inpenetrable as neither team's players could have thrown the ball into Lake Michigan much less into the basket. St. James blew us out of our own gym, 9-5, ruining our first home game in five years.

*The gym was a makeshift church in 1966-68. Now that
the school is gone, it's back to being a beautiful gym beckoning a basketball game.*

WRESTLING THE ORPHANS

Our school's gym teacher Mr. Bartstone actually had two jobs. He simultaneously headed the physical education program at both Immaculate Conception and Angel Guardian, a large orphanage some 20 miles away. With his duo position, he decided to give I.C. kids a taste of real competition for a change.

So, he decided on a school-wide competition in wrestling: Sixth-, Seventh- and Eighth Grades would face off against each other in freestyle wrestling.

Most of us at I.C. didn't know any more about wrestling than we did about quantum physics, but Bartstone was determined to put on a wrestling competition.

Since Immaculate Conception didn't have any wrestling mats, the event was slated for a Saturday at Angel Guardian.

Bartstone explained to all kids of both schools that he was neutral, and that he would root for both schools' kids to do well. He went on a recruiting drive at I.C. to fill the weight classes.

Bartstone went after me immediately, telling me I was on the list to wrestle at 85 pounds.

While I was a good wrestler, I had no intention of spending my Saturday hanging around some orphanage wrestling in one of Bartstone's concocted events.

The gym teacher insisted that I be there, and added that my opponent already had been chosen at Angel Guardian. He explained that it wouldn't be right to deprive another young man the chance to compete. I begged to differ. I wanted nothing more than to disappoint him. I'd rather stay home and cut the grass than spend the day on the road in some dank gym somewhere.

Bartstone then used his psychology against us. He told us that he doubted any of us pansies could beat any of the "men" at Angel Guardian. He even promised a wrestling trophy and a patch to anyone who won his individual match.

Now he had my attention. After nine years of schooling at I.C., I hadn't won as much as a pencil. Suddenly, here was my chance to actually win a trophy and patch. Just for wrestling some kid my weight. I was used to wrestling kids much bigger than me, and doing well. I figured whoever was my weight had to be some scrawny kid that I could whip with one hand behind my back.

He picked us out and challenged us, personally. He told us the name of each of our respective challengers, and he said he told each Angel Guardian orphan our names, too. He explained how men for decades in our country had been brave and gone to war to meet challenges and to overcome incredible odds. Bartstone gave us the best Knute Rockne speech he could, but it still wasn't enough for me.

I had my excuse all ready for Bartstone on the day before the big match. When I told him that I couldn't attend Angel Guardian because I had to go with my mother to a shower, he laughed in my face.

"That's bullshit," he said. "Showers are for women!"

"Women?" I asked, surprised that my contrived excuse was blowing up in my face.

"Yes, showers are for women only," Bartstone said with his face up to mine. "What are you, a lady?"

"Well, I ain't going to no shower if it's for women," I declared, puffing out my chest. " I don't care what my mother says, I'm wrestling!" I proclaimed with as much bravado as a shower dodger could muster.

"Good," he replied. "Be on the bus at 8:30 a.m. tomorrow in front of the school. And good luck."

That Saturday morning, I.C.'s "Loretto" school bus was loaded up with our neophyte grapplers in the sixth-, seventh- and eighth grades. When we arrived at the expansive orphanage, it looked like a prison compound. We were ushered out of the bus and led to the locker room in the gymnasium where we changed into shorts and T-shirts.

Twenty minutes later, we were lined up across the largest wrestling mat I had ever seen, looking across at our opposite number—the kid we were going to wrestle. Bartstone, ever the sportsman, and serving as the referee, had us shake hands with our competitor then return to the sidelines and wait for our match to be called.

Immediately each of us knew why Bartstone had thought of the Angel Guardian kids as men. THEY WERE MEN! Half of their eighth grade wrestlers had beards and mustaches, for chrissakes. And suspiciously, every one of them was at least a sack of potatoes heavier than our guys.

From the time Bartstone blew the first whistle, the mismatches were apparent. Our sixth grade got destroyed. The only I.C. kid to win his match was Peter Lemke, the kid who lived across the street from me.

Our seventh grade wrestlers were tossed around like rag dolls by their bigger and older opponents. It was clear that some of those Angel Guardian kids didn't have birth certificates, because some of them looked old enough to drive. After two grades wrestled, only one I.C. kid had earned a trophy and patch.

Our eighth grade was pretty much demoralized before it even began wrestling, watching the other I.C. kids being used as dust mops on the Angel Guardian mat.

At I.C., Joe Landry was pretty much regarded as the toughest kid around. We couldn't dream of him losing, until we saw the guy Bartstone matched him up with. I was afraid for Landry's life when I saw what looked like somebody's father taking him on. Landry put up a great battle, but he was pinned in the second period.

Whatever "air" was left in our figurative balloon had all but escaped when Don Mintori was thrashed by someone who looked like his uncle.

When I was called up to the mat, I realized that my opponent was taller than me. I'd never met any kid my weight whom was taller than me, so I knew he had at least five pounds on me.

When Bartstone blew his whistle to start my match, my opponent and I tiptoed around the mat, getting the feel for each other like two guys who would rather be somewhere else.

I then realized how competitive the rest of the Angel Guardian kids were, circling the mat. They yelled encouragement to their wrestler constantly, barking out instructions, and willing their wrestler toward victory.

It was the first time I can ever remember being afraid to lose. My side of whipped I.C. kids was quiet with the exception of Ray Gracie, who had won his match on a walkover. I could hear him yelling for me to pound my opponent, even through the din of the Angel Guardian contingent.

I swept down low and captured the gangly kid's leg and tripped the remaining one on the mat for a takedown. I spun on top of him to the horror of the Angel Guardian onlookers. As I clenched the kid in a half nelson and dominated him on the mat, his cohorts turned on him.

While my opponent struggled desperately to avoid the shame of losing to a pathetic Immaculate Conception kid, I continued applying the pressure to pin his shoulders to the mat.

Bartstone sensed the inevitable. His whistle in place, he stuck his nose down by the kid's shoulder, watching his back gradually flatten to the mat. I could hear the shouts of disgust coming from his classmates.

"Get up, Montaine, you pussy, get up!"

"Don't you get pinned, you fucking dipshit!"

"None of us lose! Ever! Get up!"

"You lose and I'm kicking your ass!"

The kid's face was shear horror as he struggled to get loose. As his shoulders neared the mat and his energy sapped, tears welled in his eyes. The nearby shouts turned into screams as his teammates cursed at him in shame.

I thought about this opponent under me who had at some time lost his parents and family, now was about to lose his friends —at my hands.

He gave one, last frantic exertion trying to free himself from an ignominious defeat, but I held him off. I leaned my shoulder into his and the coup de grace was complete.

Bartstone slammed the mat with his hand and blew the whistle, signifying a pin. I jumped to my feet, now the second I.C. kid in two hours to win a wrestling match. My Angel Guardian opponent, amid the scorn of his fellow wrestlers, drooped his head in sorrow.

As Bartstone raised my hand while holding my opponent's at waist level, the Immaculate Conception wrestlers reveled with glee. I returned to our sidelines to a rejuvenated group of jumping and slapping teammates.

The celebration didn't last long, however, as the rest of the Angel Guardian orphans pounded the christ out of our guys.

I realized there was a profound difference in the way the two schools wrestled that day. Immaculate Conception kids experienced mano-a-mano competition for the first time, in a personal battle that was about nothing more than the sport of it. The Angel Guardian kids wrestled for their pride and their dignity. Their family was each other. The wrestling match was like every other day—them against the world.

When the slaughter was over, we headed back to the bus for the long ride home. To my amazement, however, my teammates—all three grades of thrashed wrestlers—were upbeat and jolly. We laughed and chuckled all the way home. Nobody was despondent over losing. After all, it was our first and last wrestling match. Against some local college, we joked.

"It's just like Bartstone to set us up," said Mintori. "Our winners get a trophy and a patch. Their guys get to keep their scholarships!"

President Kennedy was an American hero in 1961-63. Even as a kid, I admired him. I remember most his wit and intelligence. And how proud and invincible the country seemed to be, with him as leader.

NOVEMBER 22, 1963

No day in my nine years of schooling at Immaculate Conception sticks out as vividly in my mind as November 22, 1963.

My fourth grade class droned on as usual with Sister Michael Ann at the helm. I sat in the middle row about five seats back, anticipating the coming weekend. With lunch over, our class was quietly progressing through our studies, when the principal, Sister Eileen, tapped her microphone over the intercom, a subtle warning signal that she was about to speak.

As each kid instinctively looked up and watched the built-in speaker in the room, the principal spoke to us in a troubled voice. I'll always remember exactly what she said, word for word.

"Teachers and students, this is Sister Eileen. I have some bad news. President Kennedy has been shot down in the streets of Dallas, Texas..."

Every kid in the class was stunned, knowing the implications of this event, even at nine years old. Sister Michael Ann maintained her cool, and explained that class would be dismissed shortly.

My fourth-grade mind played out the scenario described by the principal.

"Shot down in the streets of Dallas, Texas" resounded in my head as my brain began writing the mental screenplay for me to comprehend.

Sitting at my desk, just after the announcement, I formulated the entire picture.

I envisioned Dallas as the wild west, a setting stuck in the 1850s. I pictured President Kennedy in a suit and tie coming out the swinging doors of a saloon onto a wooden sidewalk. As the doors swung closed behind him, he passed a horse trough and a tethering post, and walked down three wooden steps to a dirt street. As horse-drawn carriages and a stagecoach passed by, some ornery sidewinder approached.

Like Matt Dillon in the opening scene of Gunsmoke, the day's most popular TV show, the outlaw drew his gun from his holster and shot President Kennedy down in the street of Dallas, Texas.

I imagined the popular president, my hero even at nine years old, face down in the dirt as the boots and spurs of a crowd gathered around him.

As our class was solemnly dismissed from class by about 2 p.m., there was an eery silence throughout the school. It was like every kid and teacher took a punch to the stomach at the same time. It wasn't important any more if every kid was perfectly in line or if someone was talking to his neighbor. We could have chewed all the gum we wanted and blown bubbles ta boot, for all the nuns cared at that point.

There was no precedent for this turn of events at Immaculate Conception. At least not in my lifetime.

For years, the nuns had prepared us for every eventuality. We practiced crouching under our desks in survival mode to withstand Khruschev's nuclear attack. We lined up in the hallways sitting with our heads between our legs preparing to weather a Midwest tornado.

But nobody could have prepared us for the trauma that would follow our president's assassination.

While waiting my turn that day to board the bus for home, I stood outside of the principal's office window. It was a chilly but sunny day. Unable to see inside due to the height of the window, I grabbed a hold of the concrete window sill and repeated jumped up and down to gradually determine the time on the principal's wall clock. It read 2:15 p.m.

The height of that windowsill forever remained a sort of water mark for me, giving me perspective of my age and size at the time of John F. Kennedy's assassination. Only a child or a midget would need to jump to see through the principal's window.

HAMMERS, ANVILS AND HORSESHOES

The keystone to being a good Catholic, according to the nuns' teaching, was self-sacrifice. They taught us that the more we deprived ourselves, the better the Lord would like us. The more we suffered, the more we assured ourselves eternal bliss in the afterlife.

I learned that this was even true in Catholic hospitals, where nuns also show a high tolerance for other people's pain. Up through the 1960s, it was prudent for pregnant women to avoid any hospital room that was appointed with a crucifix on its wall. Nuns who double as nurses, are well known for their belief that patients' pain is a good thing, and related somehow to Godliness.

Every definition of a nun, from Webster through Funk and Wagnall's, describes a woman of a religious order who vows poverty, chastity and obedience. The reality of it is, they vow these deprivations on kids! Take a closer look at these three requisites of being a nun:

Poverty: At Immaculate Conception, the nuns were essentially the hostesses of a gulag, one that featured all the amenities and services that you'd expect to find from a first-class, Siberian prison camp. It was the students that lived the poverty aspect of nunhood, not the nuns. These Darth Vadar-costumed freeloaders lived a life that many people would love to have. The nuns were afforded gainful employment, free eats, free sleeps, free medical care, free retirement benefits, and access to an endless litany of children for their slapping pleasure.

Chastity: A nun by definition is as sexless as an amoeba. She doesn't deprive herself of sex when she becomes a nun. A would-be nun already has the makings of a human paramecium, a sexless existence by choice in her everyday life. A dead giveaway of a nun in the making is a woman riding a bicycle with her legs crossed. Society has already spurned these women for one reason or another. The church is a nun's means of escaping a society that doesn't conform to her liking. Nuns by definition are anti-social dissidents who swim upstream while the rest of society tries to make it downstream.

Nuns' natural instinct is to try to convert the whole world into paramecium animals that preferably breed exclusively in petri dishes. They couldn't stand the sight of boys and girls together, at any time. I.C.'s nuns detached boys from girls like a chef separates yolks from egg whites. The nuns' discouragement of any sort of social contact between the two genders was clear evidence of their anti-social agenda.

Obedience: The nuns vowed to make us obedient. Each kid at I.C. obeyed like a sled dog, or suffered the wrath of the nuns' figurative whip. I have no idea who the nuns obeyed. Supposedly, the bishop. Well, I'll bet I.C.'s nuns never saw a bishop in their whole life outside a chessboard. I can't imagine a bishop visiting a convent without being held at gunpoint. Being surrounded by two dozen cloaked nuns is no picnic.

Sure, there were good nuns—somewhere, I admit. Mother Teresa was a good nun. Of course, you had to go to India to find her at work during most of her lifetime. Some people question my criticism of nuns by claiming they're all not that bad. I always ask these doubters to name me one good nun. They can't. Fictitious nuns don't count. Like Sister Bertrille, the Flying Nun. That's Sally Field. Not the Singing Nun of "Dominique" fame, either. She was no more a nun than was Glenn Campbell. You can't claim "Blue Nun" either; that's a wine. Senator Nunn doesn't count, either.

I've heard stories about good nuns who used to be at Immaculate Conception before being mustered out, probably to some detention camp for wayward Sisters of Loretto. My older sister Darlene accounts for a few good nuns such as Sister Ann Carmel, a nun with whom she maintained communication for forty years.

To me, these accounts of benevolent I.C. nuns are myths. I believe them with the same veracity as I believe ghost stories. Shocking, but there's no proof. I've heard people's stories of sweet, caring I.C. nuns who took a personal interest in kids' lives or helped them overcome learning disabilities. To me these accounts are figments of delirious or over-zealous imaginations. The nuns I knew didn't relieve pain, they caused pain. They weren't part of the solution, they were part of the problem.

Pious Catholics think of nuns fondly as "Angels on Earth." Poppycock. Our nuns made the motorcycle thugs, Hell's Angels, seem like Charley's Angels.

Sure, I acknowledge that the nuns molded us to learn our studies and the ways of Catholicism. My objection is exactly that: from childhood through adolescence the nuns molded us. Not like Auguste Rodin finessely sculpted a masterpiece out of marble. The nuns pounded us like a blacksmith molds a horseshoe. At Immaculate Conception, the school was the anvil, the nuns were the hammers, and the students were the horseshoes. And when you're a horseshoe, you better get used to being stepped on. Maybe kicked a few times, too.

A nun in a crosswalk was like shooting fish in a barrel.

FIRST DAY OF SCHOOL

Life pretty much starts with the first day of school. A kid is basically an anchor around his mother's neck until the day he's able to be on his own for a few hours a day.

I heard the family pep talk for months building me up for the first day of school. Everyone talked about how much I was going to love it. Things to do, people to see, experiences to enjoy. The way my family talked, I was moving away to Disneyland for the next 12 years.

I bought into the propaganda that Immaculate Conception was going to be Shangri-lai, but I had no idea what to expect. I'd never been to the school, or any school before. Never saw a nun up close before, though I had seen them from afar in church as a tyke. Even then, they looked spooky to me.

My mother explained the plight of the nuns to me, but it was still head-scratching logic to me.

What purpose do they serve looking ridiculous like that, I wondered, even as a young squirt. I was told that their habits were part of their sacrifice. They were depriving themselves as an offering to God.

And God likes this outfit? He prefers people in repulsive, black costumes? He figures these nuns shrouded in mourning apparel relate better to other people than if they were in business suites, jeans or hot pants?

My child logic told me that if they were going to sacrifice with their clothing, why not wear suits of armor? Or chain mail, like Ivanhoe. Then, people would love them. They'd be like super-heroes.

Didn't matter. I was told that the nuns were holy ladies and they were to be respected with reverence at all times. I figured I could go along with that.

On that precipitous morning, my mother loaded me into the car and drove off toward the school four miles away. I sat in the car like a dog going to the vet for the first time. To me, we were going bye-bye, and wherever we ended up it was going to be great. Little did I realize the chain of events that were about to unfurl over the next nine years, beginning with this car ride.

My life would never be the same.

My mother tried to hold my hand but I wouldn't have it as we walked into the school and headed past the principal's office to the end of the hallway where the kindergarten room was located.

The first thing I noticed was the little white porcelain drinking fountain outside the kindergarten about two feet off the floor. It was the first drinking fountain I'd ever seen that was within my reach. I immediately went toward it and took a drink from the salient, shiny, steel mouthpiece, a devise that over the years probably resulted in more dentist bills that rock candy.

My mother pointed out that this kindergarten was where I'd be every day. She repeated that all I had to do was walk down this hall to the classroom after getting off the bus. Sounded simple to me.

The kindergarten room had high, horizontal windows that ran half the width of the room, allowing giants over five feet tall to look inside. My mother had her hand on my back gently pushing me forward toward the door just in case I made a break for it, I guess. But I wasn't afraid. I was eager to see this Disneyland of academia that everyone had been talking about.

I grabbed the big, round doorknob and heaved open the heavy wooden door. Inside were several kids my age milling around aimlessly. Immediately upon our entering, Mrs. Joycer, the kindergarten teacher, came over and welcomed us. My mother did the introducing, calling me Richard instead of my household name, Rick.

The only time I had heard myself called Richard was when my mother was mad at me. e.g. "Richard, you get yourself upstairs and pick up your dirty clothes right now. I'm not your maid around here!"

It was curious to me why she chose to refer to me as Richard. Was she mad at me? She didn't seem mad. In fact, she seemed downright happy. Too happy. Wait a minute. Is this a trick? Hey, what's going on, here?

As my mother started to slip out the door, I realized I was about to be on my own in this place. Just me, this Mrs. Joycer lady, and this motley group of toeheads wandering around. My mother said she'd see me at lunchtime and not to worry. Just have fun.

"I'll watch you through this window," mother promised. She meant the vertical window about the size of a three-foot, two-by-four, because she couldn't see through the towering horizontal windows any more than I could.

Mrs. Joycer patted me on the head and gave me a quick tour of the joint. First, the funny-opening, bi-fold closets where I'd hang my coat and lay my boots in the wintertime.

Then I saw the slanted blackboards with the holes in the bottom, and the long, weird erasers. The teacher showed me how the blackboard lifted up to provide storage space. That was cool.

We walked between a couple dozen little chairs and one big, gigantic chair to get to the built-in goldfish pond. This was the neatest thing I'd ever seen. Kids were sitting on the edge of the raised pond, watching a few paralyzed fish in the corner.

Behind us was this giant slide. I couldn't believe my eyes. A real slide in doors! I saw a kid come down the slide like a dope, hardly moving as his PF Fliers were rubbing against the aluminum, preventing a slick ride. I envisioned my first run down this giant, indoor slide. I figured I'd slide right off and across the room on my back, mowing down kids like bowling pins.

Mrs. Joycer showed me this big wooden sandwich board with a clown painted on it and wide holes at places on the clown to throw beanbags through. I loved this game. Even at five years old, I had a good arm developing. I could throw a bean bag hard and overhand like a pitcher while most kids were still flipping the bags underhand and uncoordinated.

The teacher had to abort our little tour when some little girl started crying. As Mrs. Joycer comforted the kid, another girl began to cry. Then some boy began to have a fit. In the meantime, another mother showed up at the door with her child, who was greeted by the sight of three wailing kids inside. I stood there looking at this sudden turn of events. The new kid to the room turned and clenched onto her mother as if she were about to be thrust into the rim of a volcano.

Mrs. Joycer kept her cool and her smile as she calmed all the kids at once by distracting them with a stupid blow toy, the ones you get at New Year's Eve.

As the children's insurrection was quelled, I thought I'd take a peak outside the vertical window to see how my mother was doing in the hallway. The window was so narrow I couldn't see her. So, I opened the door for a better look, and Mrs. Joycer came running over, panicking.

"Don't go outside! You can't leave. You need to stay inside, okay?" She closed the door before I could get the thing fully opened. "Go play now," she implored, "that's a good boy."

What's the big idea, I thought. I was just going to look out in the hall. It's not like I was going to bolt outside, flag down a cab and head uptown, for chrissake.

That's when I first got the inkling that there was going to be more to this place than daytime Disneyland.

After a few hours of Mrs. Joycer's biggest nightmare—the first day of school—we were lined up and marched to the front of the school where the buses would ferry us home.

This is where the organization fell apart for Mrs. Joycer and for me. I didn't know which bus to take that would get me home, the Mary or the Loretto. But luckily for me, Cheryl Lenz was alongside me. She lived right down the street from me, so, I knew whatever bus she got on, it was the right one for me.

Cheryl caught my eye and grinned silently at me, and I grinned at her as we simultaneously boarded the Loretto, homeward bound. Armando was the bus driver, and since he spoke English with an accent, he was scary to talk to. So Cheryl and I sat in different seats, all the while keeping an eye on each other.

The bus rumbled through its route, with kids getting off at their stops. Before I knew it, the bus was nearly empty and Cheryl still hadn't budged. When the final kid bounced down the steps through the folding bus doors, I began to panic. Cheryl looked at me inquisitively, and I shrugged my shoulders. Looking out the window, I could have been in Boston, for all I knew. Nothing was familiar.

Armando, turned around in his driver's seat, and looked at us, somewhat pissed off.

"Why didn't you two get off the bus?" he said in his Sicilian accent.

We were both mute and in a trance, and a little scared. At that point, I was so glad Cheryl was there with me. I knew at least we were lost together. Besides, I didn't feel so dumb with her in the same boat with me.

"Where do live?" asked the inconvenienced bus driver.

"Burton Avenue," I said.

"Ah, Jesus," he mumbled. "How 'bout you?" he asked, looking at Cheryl.

"Me, too," she uttered.

"Yeah, well, you're both on the wrong bus. Don't you know what bus you're supposed to be on?" he lectured, upset at two five year olds for making a mistake that thousands of adult Americans make in the big cities every day.

"Well, I have to take you back to school and you'll need to call your parents. I don't have time for this nonsense," he groused.

While Armando made a federal case out of the error, I wondered what the next step was. I didn't know where a phone was, and I surely didn't have a dime to make a phone call. Thank God Cheryl was with me or I'd be a goner, I thought.

As Armando swung the Loretto around the semi-circle driveway of the school, he opened the door to our welcoming committee. Cheryl and I walked down the steps of the bus like two astronauts greeted by a crowd of enthusiastic people, including our parents, a few teachers and a few other people I didn't know.

I glanced at Cheryl as she was being hugged by her mother and while I was being embraced by mine. Everyone acted as if our lives were in danger and we had been rescued right before going over Niagara Falls or something.

1959 TO 1968

Each grade at Immaculate Conception was a monumental hurdle for each student. The nuns never let you forget that they could flunk you in a Vatican City heartbeat, despite your passing grades. For any indiscretion or peccadillo, they could label you for summer school or hang the ignominious fate of flunking on you, requiring you to repeat the same grade next year.

Each grade introduced us to a new nun or teacher who would be our mentor, our fool; our friend, our foe; our leader, our lackey; our trusted confidant, our treasonous traitor.

It was never lost in our minds, not for a moment, that our nun or lay teacher was a part of the system. They represented the establishment. The lords of the manor. We were the plebians, without status or privileges other than to do what we were told.

The best we students could hope for was to spend our days as inconspicuous as we could. When the spotlight was on us, we learned to duck first and ask questions later.

The kindergarten classroom. An augury of things to come.

KINDERGARTEN

I was way above the curve in kindergarten in some respects, and way under the curve in others. When it came to motor skills, I was unsurpassed. I could fire a beanbag across the room and knock a lamp over better than any kid my age.

One day, a group of women looking official and all, came in to give us a coordination test. I remember them being amazed at my fancy footwork on a little balance beam that they set up. Also, they commented that they hadn't seen any kindergartner lately able to skip backwards as well as I did. My adroitness won me a great big "E+" on some report they handed out.

I already knew how to tell time when I got to kindergarten, too, so when Mrs. Joycer sat us all in a circle and demonstrated the clock with the cardboard face and moveable hands, I was way ahead of the game.

I also learned to tie my shoes before getting to Immaculate Conception, so Mrs. Joycer was happy to have me around filling up one of the chairs in her class.

Other skills associated with kindergarten, however, had me stumped. Joe Venici and I were the only kids in the whole class who couldn't cut out our Halloween black cats from the outline on the black craft paper. No matter how hard I concentrated, I couldn't get the scissors to work. Mysteriously, Venici was as much a clod as me, even though we both had excellent agility compared to most of the other kids.

Mrs. Joycer tried in vain to explain to us how to follow the lines and keep our hands straight when cutting. Exasperated by our failure, the teacher assigned Marguerita Gusto to cut out our cats for us. After all, our parents would be coming for parents conference day, and we had to have our cats done by then.

Unbelievably, it wasn't until the end of the year when Mrs. Joycer finally realized that Venici and I were hopelessly handicapped with the safety scissors, both of us being left handed.

We took naps at 10:30 a.m., only two hours after class began. Kindergarten was only half a day anyhow. But still, it was necessary, I guess. Some kids fell asleep, for godsake, while others twitched and rustled about the entire time. I was one of the antsy ones. I think the nap was more for Mrs. Joycer than it was for us.

Cookies and milk was the high watermark of the day for us kindergartners. Mrs. Joycer enticed us with cookies like a 19th century carriage driver dangled a carrot over a mule's head. She knew that she could get the class quiet, get the kids in line, get them seated, and get their coats and boots on much easier by threatening to put the cookies away.

Kindergarten was the last year that any teacher ever implemented the reward system. Ever afterward, the punishment system prevailed.

I tried to be one of the smartest kids in Mrs. Joycer's class, and I think I probably was. At least in certain categories. I didn't want to be a dumb ass or pull a lame brain stunt like my older brother had done when he was in kindergarten. He had gone home telling my mother that the teacher required each student to bring to class "an old mailbox." My mother fretted over the assignment, not knowing how or where to come across an old mailbox without unscrewing the family's box off our house. My brother, sniveling, insisted that was his assignment for class. When my mother finally called up the teacher to question the logic of this assignment, she learned the actual requirement was "an oatmeal box" not an "old mailbox."

The kids were going to make bongo drums out of Quaker Oats boxes. What a dumb ass. I could never be that stupid, I figured.

My favorite day was Monday. That's when we had Show-and-Tell, and I put on a great show every week. Most kids brought in stupid things like their dolls, or a pogo stick or hula hoop or yo-yo. I instead brought interesting items like a large, red, plastic racecar with big black wheels that allowed you to roll it really fast on the floor. It was awesome.

I brought in my baseball glove, which was for a righthander. Despite the misfit, I wore it like a lefty anyhow, and loved it. I demonstrated backhands, forehands, grounders, pop-ups. Very impressive.

The best Show-and-Tell of all time was when I brought in my new Mickey Mouse guitar. It had a winding knob on it that gave you the option of playing it like a jack-in-the-box or strumming it like a guitar. I always opted for the strings.

When Mrs. Joycer asked me if I could play it, I quickly responded by knocking off a rendition of Elvis Presley.

"You ain't nothing but a hound dog! You ain't nothing but a hound dog!" I sang repeatedly, the only lyrics I knew to Elvis' most famous hit.

I raked the strings of the guitar and wiggled around while singing, sending Mrs. Joycer doubling off her chair in hysterics. I guess I was pretty good. Even Elvis didn't knock them off their chairs, for chrissakes!

It didn't take me long to fall in love with my first girl. She was the smartest girl in the class, and maybe the smartest girl of all time. Joellen Sableman was the teacher's pet, and she was as bouncy and smiley and confident as a kid of five could be.

Joellen helped Mrs. Joycer prepare for class exercises as if she had been through kindergarten before. Mrs. Joycer thought the sun shined on Joellen, and so did I. She was my sweetie pie each and every day.

One day, I was absent from school when the class was making hand molds. I was delighted to learn that my hand print was done for me by none other than Joellen. To think that I had my sweetie's handprint impression in a mold, painted and decorated, as if my own. Why, in some countries, that made her my concubine. I put my hand in that mold every day, just as a tourist checks Shirley Temple's handprint at Grohman's Chinese Theater.

I told everybody at home that I loved Joellen, and they all made such a big fuss about it.

"How was your girlfriend today?" my eighth grade sister would ask me. Then it was, "How's Joellen?" as if we were married and all settled in.

"Rick's got a girlfriend at school," my mother would tell my relatives. "Her name is Joellen, isn't it, Rick?" she'd add.

After a while, I realized this girlfriend thing was getting out of control and could bite me in the ass if I didn't put a stop to it. After all, it had been six months now, and I don't think I ever said a direct word to Joellen other than maybe "sorry" or "huh?"

Odds were, Joellen couldn't have picked me out of a police lineup even after several months of schooling. But I continued to adore her anonymously. My love for Joellen continued through the year until I saw her run in the playground. My affection for her went up in flames like the Hindenburg when I realized she ran like a dork. Her hands were in fists and her arms swiveled sideways across her body as she ran. Joellen's eyebrows furled in determination and her head leaned forward to maximize her aerodynamic impetus, yet her legs chugged along at a snail's pace. She ran comically, as if she were running straight uphill.

Joellen became a heartthrob of my past at that instant. It was now time for me to secretly admire some other girl.

FIRST GRADE— SISTER MARY EILEEN

By first grade, I realized that there were two types of people in the world: paste-eaters and non-paste-eaters. About half of the kids in my class were addicted to the creamy white paste that came in the round, plastic cup with the flexible red applicator on the lid.

The paste had the consistency and look of vanilla frosting. Many of the kids would scoop out a dollop of paste onto their applicators and apply the glob of the sticky stuff to their tongues. They'd start licking their gums like a dog just given a dab of peanut butter.

I would question kids like Tim O'Reily, who made a steady diet of the paper-bonding paste, on whether he had lost his mind.

"It's delicious," he'd say, defending his appetizer dip.

"It's glue, you dope. That's what they make dead horses out of!" I exclaimed. "You're eating dead horses!"

"Am not," O'Reily countered.

"Are, too," I responded, convincingly.

"You're nuts," he alleged.

"Yeah, you're all right, you paste-eater."

That's generally how every conversation went in first grade.

Sister Mary Eileen wasn't a screamer or a hitter, but she didn't allow any monkey-shining going on in class. She was my first experience with a nun, and she was a bit scary, but not enough to have you hold your breath in fear, anyhow.

You didn't want to approach her like you could Mrs. Joycer to show her your latest boo-boo. Sister Mary Eileen was a bit standoffish even to the point where a first grader could pick up on it.

Nonetheless, she was a good teacher during a critical time in a kid's life. This was Learning to Read time and Phonics time, critical academic periods, in my assessment.

Well, Sister Mary Eileen didn't accept short cuts to learning or sloppy efforts. Especially when it came to reading. And for that, I'm indebted to her for life.

My mother taught me to tie my shoes, my brother taught me to throw a ball, and my sister taught me to ride a bike. But it was Sister Mary Eileen who taught me to read. That puts her in my personal pantheon of pedagogical heroes.

Sister Mary Eileen introduced me to Dick and Jane and Spot just as millions of other kids had been acclimated. I'll never forget my first big word: "Surprise." I remember one chapter when Uncle Lorenzo sat on a porch whittling a stick with his knife. I had never heard of whittling before.

I found reading to be exciting, easy and fun. This formative year of schooling perhaps was the most important one. A kid's success at this initial level can determine his future skills. And it all boils down to the schoolteacher along with some encouragement from the parents.

Toward the end of first grade, a peculiar thing happened to me. I woke up one day to discover that my right eye had turned in, a result of being a pre-mature baby hatched and slow-cooked in an incubator. All of a sudden, I was a six-year-old Ben Turpin walking around school looking like I was about to bump into things.

My parents never talked about it to me, but when the school pictures came back, there I was, seemingly looking at a fly on my nose with my right eye while my left looked straight ahead. It's okay for lizards to have separately functioning eyeballs, but not for first-graders.

It didn't take long before I was hearing "Hey, cross-eyed!" comments in the playground at school. I came home one day and told my mother that the kids were making fun of me in the playground, and she was visibly upset. She assured me not to worry about it, and that it was all going to be fine.

I didn't know what she meant until that summer when my parents took me to the hospital to have an eye operation. I was wheeled into the operating room by several uniformed people who comforted me, and told me not to worry. I didn't really know what there was to worry about anyhow, so it was no big deal to me. They slipped a little rubber cup like a plumber's plunger over my nose and I disappeared for a while.

When I awoke, I had patches over my eyes and heard people's voices talking to me from all around the room. I didn't feel any pain, but I remember being incredibly bored. Neither my brother nor sister was allowed to visit since they were under 18, a strict hospital rule in those days. Somehow, a nurse played checkers with me despite my eye patches. We also played Guess the Thing. People would stick stuff in my hand and I'd guess what it was. I couldn't be stumped. Toothbrush. Water glass. Straw. Nickel, no, quarter. The only time I missed is when they snuck my sister into the room and she dangled her ponytail.

My mother tried too hard to comfort me when she gave me wheelchair rides through the hallways of the hospital. Nurses were confounded why I was still so sick from the gas as I vomited continually into a stainless steel bowl. Finally, after two days of wheelchair-vomiting rides, a doctor suggested that I was getting motion sickness due to my eyes being covered with bandages.

I could hear the people in the room collectively hold their breath when the doctor removed my patches after three days. As he tore off the adhesive bandages, my eyelashes stuck to the bandages thus giving my eyes a freshly plucked look. Nobody was concerned about my eyelashes. As my blurry vision gradually focused into clear detail, my wayward eye had been corrected.

Thanks to my parents and the doctors at the hospital, my eyes, at least, wouldn't give me away

as a crazy person. Unlike thousands of unfortunate kids, I wouldn't be forced to live with the social stigma of being cross-eyed.

SECOND GRADE—SISTER ROSE TIMOTHY

When I first met Sister Rose Timothy, I thought she was going to be my next girlfriend. She was a walking, talking oxymoron: a pretty nun.

Young, lean and statuesque, Sister Rose Timothy made even a second grader wonder why the hell she was masquerading around as a nun.

Whenever she talked to a kid, she bent over and looked right in the kid's face. You always looked eye to eye with Sister despite her being twice your size.

Still, she knew how to crack the whip when someone stepped out of line—literally. It seems a nun's most difficult challenge with second graders is to keep them in line. Everywhere in Catholic School is a march, even if it's to the bathroom or the drinking fountain.

Sister Rose Timothy was forever slapping kids upside the head to get them to turn around, move over, pay attention, keep moving, or shut up.

Her affection for me turned a tad sour, I think, when I befriended the toughest kid who ever went to Immaculate Conception. Bob Musgrove was a gigantic kid, about the size of a fourth grader. He was Immaculate Conception's poster boy for misbehavior, and the nuns loved jumping on his shit every day. Musgrove flunked second grade and was forced to repeat it as his classmates were promoted to the new school building, where the older kids were.

When Musgrove got older, he was a sure bet to wear pinstripes, and I don't mean with the New York Yankees. I was certain he'd be serving seven to life by the time he got to high school. In the meantime, though, I found him to be a good guy to have on my side.

One day on the playground, one of Musgrove's older, former classmates, Jim Duncan, apparently pissed him off for some reason. So Musgrove, in front of witnesses, picked up a rock and bashed it over the kid's head. I saw the back of Duncan's head bleeding profusely; the first time I had really seen decent blood drawn.

Musgrove got into big-time trouble that day, but he remained undaunted. His reputation rose to Grand High Exalted Playground Ruler. He had the third graders shaking in their collective boots. At a drop of a hat, our leftover second grader could confront any third grader who bullied us on the playground. Musgrove served as the second graders' one-man army. And I was his buddy.

One day, Sister Rose Timothy caught me and Musgrove throwing little pieces of Playdoah at other kids in the class. She made Musgrove stand in the corner with his hands on his head, but left me sitting at my desk. Only she gave me a death stare that I'll never forget. Like most nuns, she felt that my goofing around was a personal betrayal of her. From that day on, I was one of the kids she USED to like.

But she didn't understand the politics of it. I was the only kid in either grade that wasn't deathly afraid of Musgrove. In fact, I was kind of like his lion tamer. He actually listened to me, since I really was his only friend.

There was no denying it, Musgrove was as dumb as a dust mite. One time, Sister asked him a simple addition problem, like eight and five, and I watched him counting on his fingers while looking up at the ceiling. As the nun angrily berated him for being a dope, I came to his aid.

"Thirteen!" I whispered, like a ventriloquist. If I was Paul Winchell, Musgrove definitely was Knucklehead Smith.

"Thirteen, stupid!" I whispered again, until Musgrove finally spoke up with the answer.

The more I helped him, the more we bonded.

There were times when I was categorically out of my mind with overconfidence.

The huge kid would be flicking some guy's ears unmercifully in front of him and I'd say,

"Hey, leave him alone or I'll tear your tonsils out," a Moe Howard epithet that slew Musgrove.

Even in the playground, we walked around together, Musgrove parting crowds like the Red Sea. Sister Rose Timothy surprised me by keeping us sitting together in the back of the room. I later figured out that I was doing more to quell Musgrove's homicidal tendencies that any method of his punishment would produce. Somehow, I became Frank Buck to a wild tiger.

The winter often times played a role in how I got to school. One cold, wintry day, while my father took his turn car-pooling four kids, we were in an accident. About a half-mile from school, my father's Buick was smashed into by a woman driving a snow-covered car. The Buick spun around, doing a 360-degree revolution in the intersection by Lincoln school, a public grade school. The woman had blown through a stop sign and disabled our back tire.

In the freezing temperature, us school kids had no choice but to walk the rest of the way to school. In 1961, it wasn't unthinkable that kids actually walked more than 40 feet at any given time, even in inclement weather.

By the time us four kids arrived together at school, the principal, Sister Eileen, and a few aides greeted us at the door like we were the Donner party. Apparently, my father called ahead to the school to let the teachers know we were in a car accident and would be late.

My fingers were frozen stiff despite having the woven mittens with the spring-loaded clips latched on to my sleeve, as was common for forgetful kids like me. My nose was red and running and my eyeballs were nearly frozen in their sockets. The sudden heat of the school building made my hands and feet burn as they thawed.

Sister Rose Timothy wrapped her arms around me as if to stimulate blood through me, and walked me over to the radiator as if I were in a shipwreck. The compassion exhibited by three nuns within three minutes scared me. I eventually found out that I'd never experience that type of "fear" ever again.

THIRD GRADE—
MRS. SEZZO

If Mrs. Sezzo lived in the Mesozoic era, she'd be the indomitable, flesh-eating Tyrannosaurus Rex.

Sezzo's reputation preceded her, as every kid in the school had heard the rumors of the vicious, unmerciful tyrant that taught unfortunate third graders.

She didn't take long laying down the law in her classroom. There'd be no talking, no turning around, no shenanigans whatsoever. And if everything was going fine, she'd find a way of picking on somebody to break the peace.

One morning, as the class stood for prayers, Sezzo positioned herself in the middle of the room to survey the students. Dan Volare and I were in the middle of the first row with our backs turned to Sezzo as we addressed the statue of the Virgin Mary. As our the class audibly recited its morning prayers in unison, we all waited to see who Sezzo would pick on upon our completion.

As we all sat down, Sezzo started in with her nagging.

"Well, Volare, you only bothered to say 'Amen' and Philip, you didn't bother to say anything!"

From where she was standing, the old battle axe wasn't able to see whether we were saying our prayers or not. It was her way of saying good morning to us, personally.

She loved to call me "Philip," a derivation of my last name. The entire year, she called me "Philip," her way of slapping me in the face.

When parents' conference came around, I prepared my mother and father for their encounter with the diabolical Mrs. Sezzo. They pooh-poohed it as a figment of my imagination. Surely I was exaggerating about the surly old crow, they figured.

I had visions of Sezzo bitching to my parents about my not saying my prayers loud enough or talking to my neighbor, or not picking up my feet when I walked, shit like that. Instead, my parents came home raving about what a wonderful woman she was. I insisted they got lost and went into the wrong room, or sat down with an impostor.

"What did Sezzo say about me?" I asked, still doubting that they'd talked to the genuine Mrs. Sezzo.

"She likes you, " my mother stated. "She thinks you're a fine boy."

"What?! You're kidding! Sezzo said that?" I queried. "She says you do good work, but need to improve your study habits."

Incredible. That's not the same woman I sit down with every single day. Again, I tried to convince my parents that this woman is Ghengis Khan in sheep's clothing, but the more I talked, the more I lost credibility. They weren't buying it.

"One last question," I asked my parents. "Did Sezzo call me 'Philip'?"

"She called you Richard. I'm telling you, she likes you," my father insisted.

"And I'm telling you she's Frankenstein in seemed hose," I said.

One day, Sezzo sensed that I was stuck on a math problem, so she called me to the board to make me sweat it out in front of an audience.

I stood at the board studying the problem to no avail, then turned back to look at the class. It was the first time I had ever been to the front of the class and experienced the teacher's point of view of the kids at their desks. It was depressing. The kids looked back at me with complete disinterest. Eyelids drooped over vacant eyes that stared ahead comatose. Chins sat in chests; mouths crumbled in boredom. They all looked like a herd of cows looking stupidly over a fence.

Kids watched me struggle while the clock came to a screeching halt. Sezzo let me linger over the problem at the board in front of the excruciating audience. Unable to proceed, I hoped that either she pulled the lever to the trap door at the chalkboard and allowed me to drop away to the crocodiles, or mercifully told me to sit down. Only after I finally reached the embarrassment stage of dunce, did she allow me to take my seat, turning her psychotic attention to one of my classmates.

There was a rumor going around school in the Spring of that horrible year that Sezzo was going to teach the fourth grade the next year, thus following me to my next grade. The thought of having that witch teach me two years in a row was enough to give me birthmarks. Allah be praised, it was only a rumor.

FOURTH GRADE— SISTER MICHAEL ANN

The fourth grade was the perfect solution to an entire year of boot camp with Sezzo in third grade. Sister Michael Ann was a quiet, middle-aged disciplinarian. She didn't make a lot of noise and didn't try to humiliate students along the way as was generally the motis operandi of most nuns. She was more interested in teaching than dominating a classroom in dictatorial fashion.

Still, she was impossible to get close to. She built a figurative moat around herself prohibiting any kid from getting too much attention. Sister Michael Ann kept her students an arm's length away, almost afraid of emotional connection.

That was fine with me. I wasn't interested in recruiting any nuns to attend my next birthday party, anyway.

During the fourth grade, I noticed myself getting sweet on Ellen Mallory, perhaps the smartest kid in our class. She didn't speak much, except when spoken to, basically. But she always had the right answer when called upon, even when the rest of the class was stumped. I liked that.

Ellen Mallory had a way of looking attractive even in glasses. She squinted a bit, which was adorable to me. Plus, I never heard any guy talk about her, good or bad.

I had remarkable luck the entire year. As often as Sister Michael Ann switched kids' desks around in the room, I always stayed right next to Ellen Mallory. There was a slight problem, though. I was seated directly in front of her, in the last row by the door. Since I didn't have eyes in back of my head like a nun, I resigned to sitting sidesaddle at my desk. Occasionally, I could get a backward glance in at her, or smile during a break.

Whenever Ellen was called on, I did a 180 degree turn to get a long look at the wondrous spectacled beauty with the steel trap mind. In my usual, cowardly fashion, I withheld talking to her much, thinking she couldn't think me a fool if I didn't say anything stupid. I was way too cautious with her since she was very shy herself.

So we communicated in ridiculous ways, and managed to show a tacit sort of affection for each other. I kept track of everything she was doing behind me like I had radar. I could tell if her hands were on her desk or in her lap or in the air. I knew where her feet were, and just about what she was thinking at all times.

When Ellen dropped her pencil, I went scurrying for it as if I were a gentile suitor from the 1800s. It didn't take long for Ellen to work me like a puppet on a string. She dropped her pencil an average of 12 times a day, and I pounced on it every time, even if it rolled under someone's desk behind her. I retrieved her pencil better than any Golden Retriever could. Sometimes, I could hear her pencil rolling on her desk, and I'd catch it before it hit the ground. Not a bad feat for a guy whose back is turned.

To me, she didn't drop her pencil enough. I felt like her hero every time I returned the pencil. And she smiled at me every time.

One day, Sister Michael Ann got out the math flash cards and went around the room pitting one kid against the other. The student whom answered the flash card equation quicker, moved to the desk behind and challenged the next kid.

When it was Ellen Mallory's turn, she got on a roll, dismissing her challengers one at a time. She moved from desk to desk like a princess, never nervous and always gracious as she snapped out her correct, winning answers. She went up one row and down another, undefeated. I rooted for her to run the table, hoping she'd get to me to be her last opponent.

To the amazement and awe of the entire room, Ellen swept through the entire classroom of 30 kids, beating every one to the answer of the flash cards. Then she stepped next to my desk, the last hurdle to making it a clean sweep.

I had a dilemma to deal with. Would Ellen like me better if I beat her or prefer that I didn't beat her? I was confounded by the circumstance. I figured she'd probably beat me anyway, making it a moot point. So I decided to give it my best shot, and hope she'd be happy with the results.

Sister Michael Ann announced to the class that Ellen was just one win away from making it all the way back to her seat as a winner. I couldn't believe it, the nun was hyping my turn. Now there was pressure, too. I sure didn't want to blurt out the wrong answer, ruining Ellen's triumph by her winning the final challenge by default.

The best part was, Ellen was standing there next to me, and her right hand lie gently on my desk. We both watched intently as Sister Michael Ann prepared to present the card. The room was silent, and then the card appeared. 6x7 was the equation. It couldn't have been a better flashcard for me since I know my sevens best of all. Any kid who loves football as much as I do is going to get his sevens. After all, touchdowns are counted in sevens in the playground.

"Forty-two!" I screamed out in a millisecond, then noticed that I was the only one screaming. I won? I beat Ellen Mallory with one last seat to go? I was ecstatic inside, but non-celebrating on the outside. The nun congratulated Ellen on a remarkable performance. Nobody suspected that she may have thrown the last flashcard, allowing me to be victorious. I think I was fast enough to beat almost anybody on that occasion, but Ellen hadn't been speechless the entire run of the classroom. All of a sudden, she can't get an answer out? She might have let me win. She had the character and the confidence to do it, even as a nine-year-old fourth grader.

I proceeded to beat three more kids behind Ellen, and had visions of defeating 25 more kids and rendezvousing with her for a rematch. But reality struck, and John Sarducci jumped all over one, sending me back to my seat. I sat there silently wondering if I really beat the magnificent princess behind me, or if she gave the honor to me on a silver platter. I asked myself which I'd prefer. Would I rather know I beat the unbeatable? Or would I prefer to know that this girl liked me so much that she'd sacrifice her own accolades just so I could win?

FIFTH GRADE— SISTER AGNES MARITA

Sister Agnes Marita, otherwise known as "Lerch" to us kids, was an intimidating figure. Over six feet tall and gangly, she could send a shiver up your spine with one of her patented stares.

Nevertheless, the fear of Lerch's reprisal didn't stop our fifth-grade class from initiating a school time donnybrook that went down in the annals of Immaculate Conception as the most riotous ever.

One day, an office worker from the principal's office came to our classroom door and motioned for Sister Agnes Marita to have a word with her at the doorway. The two spoke for a few seconds before Sister told our class that she'd have to go down to the office for a few minutes. She told us to begin reading the next chapter of our history book.

Well, that wasn't likely to happen. Figuring on at least two minutes of freedom, our class didn't take long to get into a frisky mood. As soon as Lerch left the room, Mike Camden saw the opportunity to turn around and slash me with his ruler, a joy he partook in every chance he could.

I battled back with him in swashbuckling fashion with my own ruler. Throughout the room, pockets of mayhem broke out. The noise level in the room rose 20 decibels as each kid displayed his own version of being free at Alcatraz.

I saw Ray Dempster jump to his feet, grab a blackboard eraser, and scurry to the door to make sure the coast was clear. I could see he was preparing to throw the eraser at either me or Camden, so I took a two-inch piece of chalk out of my desk tray and readied to fire it at Dempster as a preemptive attack. As Dempster looked down the hall, I fired the chalk at him. As he turned around to ready his throw, the flying chalk hit him square in the forehead. If he were a Cyclops, it would have put out his eye.

The whole class burst into laughter, and the riot was on. Suddenly kids were sprinting to the blackboard dasher and breaking chalk into little throwing missiles. Dempster repeatedly clapped his eraser over Fred Belmarti's head, leaving chalk imprints all over his hair. Then he tossed the eraser across the room, hoping it would hit either Camden or me. Dempster tossed his hands over his head and ducked with guilt after his errant eraser hit angelic Marion Sculty in the skull.

As the chalk started flying across the room, kids were ducking and throwing at the same time. Anyone who got out of his or her seat became a target as flying debris made it too dangerous to move around. As Dempster turned his chalk assault on me in retribution for my direct hit to his forehead, Cynthia Keaton collected loose ammunition for me to fire return volleys.

Recruiting Cynthia to be on my side was a major coup for me, since she was easily the most popular girl in our grade. It was redundant to say that I was in love with her. Every boy that I knew had a crush on her. She was smart and cute, and had a great sense of humor. When I was lucky enough to have conversations with her, we actually had fun exchanging insults. She had a great vocabulary for derogatory badinage. We both had a self-deprecating sense of humor, too, so we had lots of laughs. Whenever I talked to her, insults notwithstanding, I realized I was talking to a queen, so I savored every syllable.

The bombardment continued all around me. Ray Gracie took bullseye carmel cremes out of his lunch bag and began pelting them at Chris Keshawn. Keshawn would eat one and throw one back. Camden took a flying eraser in the chest, then jumped out of his seat, wielding his ruler. Like a medieval knight, he began chopping and smacking random kids on the way up the aisle heading for Dempster, who saw him coming and decided to circle around the room.

Somebody flicked the fluorescent room lights on and off as the rumble continued unaffected. Kids were all over the place, standing on chairs, pushing desks aside, running up and down the aisles and throwing everything within grasp. As the riot reached its peak, everything became suspended in animation when a loud and familiar throat clearing emanated from the doorway.

Faces froze in fear and eyes bulged in terror as they saw Sister Agnes Marita's hand on the light switch, turning the lights on and off. There was nothing to hide; everyone was caught in the act. Nobody, not the most innocent girl nor the most meek boy, was behaving. It was impossible to be in that chaotic environment and not be swept along in its revoltingly wonderful pandemonium.

Lerch wasn't amused. Her eyes swept the room, burning holes into each kid along the way. Students clamored back into their seats, regardless of where their displaced desks were located. There wasn't a straight row in the classroom, as the angry nun walked around the askew desks and chairs. With her arms folded, she assessed the condition of the room. Students, in exaggeratedly good behavior, sat straight up, in sitting attention, with their hands folded on their desks. It was no time to look anything less than contrite and obedient.

The nun explained that the rest of the afternoon was going to be dedicated to cleaning the room. And she hinted that it was going to last until well after the school bell rang.

The class got punished together, and each of us was given an assignment. My job was to clean the chalkboard. Not erase the board, but clean it with a rag and some special oil that required scrubbing and buffing. Other kids had to clean the floor, scrub the desks, clean the shelves by the window and organize the supply closet.

Our class was the last to leave the school building that day. But we survived a classroom fiasco that would always be remembered by those who partook in it.

That will leave a mark! On my car!

SIXTH GRADE— MRS. MCCAFFERY

Mrs. McCaffery was a strict, slaphappy sort who flew off the handle ten times a day to take her frustration out on some vulnerable kid. The difference between Mrs. McCaffery and Mrs.

Sezzo, the diabolical third-grade teacher, was that McCaffery had an air of style and class about her.

There was no need to guess with whom she was angry when McCaffery got her shorts in a bind. She'd holler out a kid's name and then blast him with insults and derisive rhetoric.

Jeff Ralston was one of her favorite targets. He was dumb enough to be vulnerable and big and strong enough to weather even the most violent of McCaffery's attacks.

"Ralston, sit down. You want me to come down there and slap you into your seat?"

Many times, Ralston took McCaffery's slaps across the the back and head. Dave Pasqualoni was another big target, only he was a more sensitive kid. He could take McCaffery's wallops without a problem; it was the insults that got to him.

"Don't look up at the ceiling, Pasqualoni. You won't find the answer up there!"

"Maybe if you read your lessons once in a while, you wouldn't look so silly in class!"

McCaffery couldn't stand any kid not paying attention. I remember her pushing desks aside like a rhinoceros to get at Bill Kapers who was talking or daydreaming, or something. McCaffery would make a spectacle out of little things that kids did, then blame the entire class for disrupting the lecture.

Her hair-trigger temper was legendary around Immaculate Conception for twenty-five years. Some kids in my class had fathers who were taught by McCaffery. Nobody messed with McCaffery; not the principal, not the parents, not the students. If I ever had to be in a foxhole somewhere, I surely wanted to have McCaffery by my side.

She was a religious woman, and absolutely loved Notre Dame. I guess her husband and other members of her family were Golden Domers, so she had blue and gold running through her veins. Mondays were cheerful days for McCaffery when the Irish won that weekend.

Fortunately for our class, Notre Dame was on its way to building a national championship team in football until it lost and tied its last two games to Michigan State and Miami respectively. McCaffery had the entire class rooting for the Fighting Irish. We all knew that ND's success was in our best interests since McCaffery's blood pressure would be reduced to the boiling point if the South Benders won on Saturday.

McCaffery had to get Notre Dame in on the act while teaching us fractions in math. She instructed us to remember numerator and denominator by thinking of the "N" in Notre on the top and the "D" in Dame on the bottom. It worked. Of course, North Dakota could have had the same effect.

The following football year, I was tempted to go into McCaffery's class and do some friendly taunting. It was the famous title year of 1966, when Notre Dame and Michigan State played to a 10-10 tie. I contemplated teasing Mrs. McCaffery about Irish coach Ara Parseghian chickening out in the fourth quarter and playing for a tie, a really touchy subject for Notre Damers. Discretion won out over valor in my case, as well as Parseghian's. I kept the teasing to myself, realizing that a sleeping dog like McCaffery was best left undisturbed.

Despite McCaffery's volatile nature, she evoked an aura of class. She was well dressed and had her hair done up and her long nails manicured every day as if she had a live-in beautician at her disposal. She sported a big diamond ring on her finger, an object one hoped wouldn't be used to cut open a gashing wound during one of her patented slaps. She possessed a wide variety of accessories like pearls and chains and beads galore. For a woman in her early 60s, she looked dapper despite her wrinkles and bags under her eyes.

McCaffery was a caring and generous woman, too, if you looked beyond her classroom conniptions.

She nearly killed Tazmilio one day for kicking dirt off his shoes and hiding the mess under her precious, 12' x 10' rug in the classroom. McCaffery was the only teacher who had a carpet in her classroom, adding a living room effect to the setting. She made sure every kid kept that rug in prime condition. Yet, one winter day, she looked outsider her classroom window and noticed a motorist helplessly stuck in a snow pile.

Contrary to her proven obsession about the rug, she chose four boys to carry the entire carpet down to the roadway. There, coming to the aid of the motorist, McCaffery instructed the boys to spread the rug beneath the spinning, muddy wheels, providing traction for the snowed-in vehicle. The car splattered slush and mud all over the now-crumbled carpet. Along with a lot of pushing and rocking, the car finally dislodged itself from its snowy trap. The motorist gave her thanks and bid adieu as the four boys walked McCaffery's carpet over to the school's industrial dumpster.

McCaffery could teach kids valuable lessons either by a left hook or by her generosity, with equal dexterity.

SEVENTH GRADE—SISTER DANIEL MARIE

Whenever she left the room or walked down a hallway, Sister Daniel Marie was taunted with the sounds of children tooting like a ship's foghorn. After all, her nickname was "Tugboat," and the sounds were an anonymous signal that she was in the vicinity.

Tugboat seldom smiled. Her face was unaccustomed to using the dormant muscles that lifted her mouth into smiling mode. She looked a lot like Ruth Buzzi, the Laugh-In comedienne, when playing her patented, prudish, old lady persona.

In the seventh grade, the nuns decided to separate the boys and girls, avoiding any potential problems that came attached with attracting the opposite sex's attention.

Tugboat, for all her deep-seated, emotional problems and sour-puss countenance, was actually the better draw of teachers in the seventh grade.

While the boys had to endure Tugboat's hissy fits and over-reactions to daily occurrences, the girls were stuck with Sister Mary Barbara, a diminutive dictator with flaming nostrils. Despite her being smaller than every kid in her class, one couldn't help looking deep into the darkness of her wide open nose cavities.

Sister Mary Barbara was infamous for dishing out her scorn and coupling any verbal punishment with Newton-stumping math problems. I got reported to Sister Mary Barbara once for throwing a snowball at my bus stop—after school was out—by Katherine Swany, Sister's sycophantic, bus monitor. Since Sister Mary Barbara was the self-appointed judge and jury of all bus behavior, I was forced to attend bus court, a kangaroo set up in Mary Barbara's classroom after school. I pleaded that my snowball was thrown one hour after school was adjourned, off school property and at a kid who didn't even go to Immaculate Conception. Even Sister's henchgirl, Katherine Swany, agreed that the snowball wasn't thrown at the bus or anything. But the sawed off sister stuck me with an Einstein-boggling math problem to do over the weekend, anyhow.

Tugboat wasn't a thrill a minute in class, but every boy was grateful to the Lord for not having to look at "Nostrildamus" day in and day out.

For some inexplicable reason, Tugboat thought it was a good idea for the desks in our classroom to be paired up side by side. For most of the year, I was coupled with Mike Womsley, who was a master at figuring out clandestine classroom games or amusements to pass the time.

We each kept a round ball of putty in our desk, which allowed us to devise many games and contests with our desks adjoined. We played war games by molding little cannons, and lobbing putty cannon balls at each other's army. We each molded tiny golf putters and we played golf across our two desks for hours every day. Books were out of bounds and pencils were hazards.

One day, Womsley got careless, and had his head down conspicuously while he doodled on his reading workbook. A superb freehand artist, he had just drawn a great nude in pencil on his workbook when Tugboat noticed he wasn't listening.

"Michael," she bellowed. "What are you writing?" asked the irascible nun.

A danger siren screamed in both Womsley's and my head. I had to extricate Womsley out of this mess somehow or his ass was grass. If Tugboat discovered that Womsley was drawing a nude woman on his workbook, any of the following could happen:

a) Tugboat would faint at the shock

b) She'd pass the book around for all to see

c) Confiscate the workbook and show it to the principal, or

d) Save the book's cover and show it to Womsley's parents at Parents Conference Night.

None of the options were particularly favorable for a kid trying to survive Catholic School.

When Tugboat again questioned what he was writing, Womsley slyly stood and slid his workbook across to my desk, where I waited with an eraser in hand. With my head looking forward to divert any suspicion, I desperately began erasing his Rubenesque rendition.

Womsley stalled the inquisitive nun. "I'm not writing anything, sister," he claimed.

"I know you're writing something! "Bring it on up here," Tugboat demanded.

"I was just writing in my workbook," he said, buying me time to erase his exotic doodlings.

"Bring it up here this instant!" Tugboat yelled, irritated that the debate had lasted 60 seconds.

Finally, I completed the erasing and immediately slid the workbook back in front of him. He took it up to Tugboat for her inspection. She looked it over, unable to find any suspicious writing, while he stood by. The lack of incriminating evidence didn't evoke an apology from the cantankerous nun. Instead, she shifted gears and scolded him for not paying attention.

Seventh grade was the first year boys were allowed to serve on patrol. To be a patrol boy and wear the yellow shoulder and waist belt was a chance to exhibit authority and power.

Every day a half-hour before school, and five minutes before the end of school, the week's selected patrol boys would station themselves at the intersection up by the church on busy Green Bay Road, and down by the sidewalk crossing at the school's entrance.

No matter what the weather, the patrol boys would bravely do their jobs of protecting younger children from getting steamrolled by speeding or careless motorists.

Sometimes it would be zero degrees with the wind blowing hard, and the patrol boys would be at their posts, undaunted by the inclement weather.

When I was on patrol, I felt like a cop, waving kids across the street, or stretching my hands out to the sides to stop pedestrians from proceeding. We were also given the authority to stop kids from running on the sidewalk or running amuck along the roadside. When the weather got nasty, I used to think of myself as a Marine. I became an imaginary bronze star winner, fighting off frostbite, sneering in the face of Winter, like a World War II hero at Bastogne.

My best chance for glory was to get a girl—any girl—to notice me braving the weather while dodging the speeding automobiles. I fantasized about saving some third-grader's life by diving out into the street and pulling the kid to safety as a swerving, out-of-control taxicab went barreling by. The imaginary applause of the entire school at assembly was enough to keep me warm while on patrol.

Sometimes I'd question my reaction if it were Sister Mary Barbara instead of the third grader in the homicidal taxicab's crosshairs. It was a tough, hypothetical question, but I concluded that I'd have to save her. But not without administering one of my patented, pom-pom clothesline tackles.

EIGHTH GRADE— SISTER ALPHONSA MARIE

Sister Alphonsa Marie sometimes was referred to as "Groucho." Now, despite having a little mustache, an aquiline nose, and a touch of osteoporosis, she wasn't nicknamed "Groucho" because she looked or walked like Groucho Marx. She didn't smoke a cigar to the best of my knowledge, but she sure was grouchy. When she talked, and especially when she was irritated, she dropped the lids of her eyes and babbled on as if she could see right through her eyelids. To us kids, she was Groucho in nun's clothing.

Sister Alphonsa Marie was approaching retirement by the time I reached her eighth grade class. She prided herself as being the mythological dean of nuns at I.C., and she probably was smarter than the rest. If it weren't for her grousing all the time, her class might have been enjoyable. Her humor was like all I.C. nuns—deprecating. She found great humor and satisfaction in sarcasm. No kid could escape it. By the eighth grade, however, we'd all grown inure to the criticism of nuns.

For all Groucho's intelligence, however, she was pretty naive. Our eighth grade boys pulled one over on her the entire year. Or so we think. Sister Alphonsa Marie hated to grade tests, especially quizzes. But she loved to give them. This trait was one of the great ironies of Sister Alphonsa Marie and several other nuns at I.C., too. They were pleased to assign work, yet less enthusiastic to grade the work.

Groucho must have figured that she'd discovered the antidote to test grading. She simply had each kid hand his paper to the person to the left. Those seated in the far left row, brought their papers over to those students sitting in the first row on the right. Each student would grade the paper of another student, yet students didn't exchange with each other. Sister Alphonsa Marie figured she would avoid any reciprocal cheating by students who decided to turn a blind eye toward each other's paper.

So, every other day or so, Groucho had a pop quiz in one subject or another. Maybe History one day; Spelling another; English another. The beautiful part for her was, all she had to do was read off the correct answers one at a time, and let the students grade their own papers. When all the answers were given, each student grading a neighbor's paper totaled up the number wrong and logged a grade. Sister then read each kid's name from her grade book. The student who graded the paper of the kid called, would state out loud his grade.

To make everything kosher, Alphonsa Marie had the papers passed up the rows to the front of the class. That way, no test giver ever got his test back. Sister could quickly check to be sure that the graders did a correct job of calculating, and that was all there was to it. Nice job for her. No grading of tests.

The only thing is, the boys were ready for Sister Alphonsa Marie's system and devised a way to break it. Most boys conspired to exchange pens and/or pencils with their test grader. It was the buddy system at its best. Out of 30 boys in the class, perhaps 24 participated in the Buddy Forging System using the test-taker's original pen.

So, if you didn't know the answer to one of Groucho's questions, the general rule of thumb was to leave it blank and let the grader fill in the answer for you.

We knew it was tricky business filling in answers and cheating on quizzes right under Sister Alphonsa's nose. If even one kid got caught, we'd all be in deep shit. So, we all maintained discipline and remembered our motto: "Greed killed the pecker." That meant, don't get greedy and push for an "A" all the time. Each student was expected to seek the grade that was usually within his grasp, to avoid suspicion.

Dave Pasqualoni was smart enough to be happy with a C or C+. Kevin O'Brien sought a C+ or B. Others sprinkled in an "A" with their "Bs."

Each grader knew the level of the student whose paper he was grading. After all, most of us were in the ninth year of school together. Sister Alphonsa Marie hadn't calculated the strength of the boys' bond or the students' ability to cooperate independently and randomly with each other.

Each boy mastered his own skill of slyly filling in answers on the test they were grading without looking like they were doing so. It helped that Alphonsa Marie's eyesight was augmented by bifocals that magnified her eyes like Fearless Fly. She wasn't looking out into the class much while reading off the correct answers to the quizzes. It gave us plenty of opportunity to "massage" our buddy's test answers.

Our clandestine, buddy grading system went on all year long without being detected by the erudite nun. After all the sarcasm and all the bullshit we absorbed from the nuns over the years, I wonder if we actually got the final laugh.

Fred Belmarti almost fell victim to what our motto warned against: "Greed." By virtue of my brother being an 8th grade school teacher in another suburban Catholic school, I had managed to abscond a teacher's English manual. The specially prepared publication, for teachers only, looked just like a student's workbook except it featured all the correct answers in italics. The value of this book was priceless, saving me countless hours of researching for correct answers to satisfy the crummy workbook questions.

Knowing the yearlong value of this book, I couldn't risk letting a bunch of boys in on the secret. I told Fred Belmarti only, and allowed him to borrow the manual whenever there was an assignment from it.

Alphonsa Marie graded the tests at the end of each chapter, and Fred and I were sitting pretty with the teacher's answers. I warned Fred not to get an A+ on every test, since some of the answers were difficult even for John Lorrenzo or John Sarducci. To be sure, Fred wasn't on his way to becoming a National Honor Society candidate, so I told him to be modest.

As we progressed through the chapters, Fred was getting an "A" almost every week. He was putting down answers using words that he didn't even know the meaning of. I finally had to threaten to refuse his access to the manual if he didn't pull back on the reins.

Belmarti continued to do better than his average, and so did I. It was a miracle we didn't get caught. It just proved how lazy and careless Sister Alphonsa Marie had gotten. Almost as careless as Belmarti. I looked over one of Fred's chapter tests that he got returned from Sister. One of the questions had an extremely dubious answer. To my horror, the dope had written as his response, "Answers May Vary."

Last day of school always made the nuns smile.

LAST DAY OF SCHOOL

By the time June had arrived, eighth graders were already mentally checked out of Immaculate Conception. While some kids were never really checked in, I.C. was a fete accompli weeks before school was officially out. We all felt like inmates just waiting those final calendar days before being paroled.

The relative freedom and independence of high school beckoned like a ringing bell. The thought of never seeing a nun again in a classroom gave me goose bumps. There were no misty eyes on that final day of school. We took a few exams earlier in the week. This abbreviated day was reserved for handing out report cards and bidding farewell. Sister Alphonsa Marie nodded to a few kids in her condescending way, and said good luck to everyone. She shuffled through papers on her desk as the boys in her class shook hands with each other and laughed about their figurative chains being removed.

Alphonsa Marie peered over her bi-focals as her students gradually emptied the room. One more year drifted away from her own life as she watched another year's worth of kids disseminate to the future's shore like a batch of freshly hatched turtles.

As I walked out of Alphonsa Marie's class for the last time, I couldn't resist turning back for a look over my shoulder. I knew I was dropping the proverbial curtain on this part of my life. I waited a long time for this final look, and now it was here. I wanted to paint this picture in my head forever. As I locked in the vision, I realized that this was no masterpiece worth preserving for a lifetime. But I suppose I did anyway.

Over my shoulder, I saw Alphonsa Marie seated at her desk, head down and writing, presumably busying herself for something important. But she was faking. Our report cards were already done and handed out. The ball game was over and the fans were heading to the parking lot to get on with their life. It was easier to look busy than to say good-bye.

Looking at the aging nun as I moved away was the first time I ever thought about never seeing someone again. I knew I'd never go back. For what? Why would I ever see Alphonsa Marie again? Inmates don't go back to Levenworth to visit the guards that held them captive and deprived them of simple privileges. There were no good times to reminisce over. We had no rapport. She never even tried to establish a bond; only bondage. The nuns like Alphonsa Marie choose a life of restriction and deprivation, then try to espouse that lifestyle on everyone else around them. They are shells with their insides stolen away.

As I took my last step within view of the classroom, I saw her lift her head for a peek. It was too late for a nod, but she knew at least I looked back.

I threw open the outside door of the school building and danced down the concrete stairs. The sky was blue and the air was fresher than I had ever smelled it before. I filled my lungs with a giant breath of sweet life and walked up the sidewalk toward my destiny.

Then, as if I were tapped on the shoulder, I turned around to look at the school building. In the second-floor classroom at the far east side, I saw a figure in the window. I shaded my eyes with my right hand to be sure of what I was seeing. Sister Alphonsa Marie was waving to me. It was a cathartic moment. This was the image I'd hold onto for a lifetime. This was the masterpiece, the Rembrandt of a final memory. This last ditch, human emotion escaping Sister Alphonsa Marie didn't go unnoticed or unappreciated. While walking backwards and watching her, I waved farewell with a smile, then turned and ran up the hill one last time.

THE DREAMS

I still have dreams of Immaculate Conception and those days of academic detention. In my dreams, my classmates are frozen in time, forever children. Their personalities are unchanged. They are all actors in a play that was my childhood, school experiences. They all have roles. Some are stars. Others have character roles. Some have mere bit parts. It's interesting that the scriptwriter and director of my dreams does not play favorites when it comes to assigning actor roles. Sometimes an entire dream can star a classmate of mine who played only a bit part in my actual life. I can't count how many times Stanley Lang enters my dreams. Kids that I haven't seen since they left kindergarten return to take a place in my dreams of Immaculate Conception.

I dream of Mrs. Sezzo and the nuns, but not the way I'd expect. If I were in fact the executive producer of my dreams, there would be all kinds of retribution going on. My third-grade classmates surely would be taking turns giving Mrs. Sezzo atomic wedgies. One at a time, the nuns would be sent through a gauntlet of I.C. kids, crawling through our legs as we formed a human spanking machine.

The dream of tossing a banana cream pie in the puss of Sister Mary Barbara has never made it to celluloid in my cinematic, nighttime illusions. Not once have I pulled the veil off Sister Michael Ann, uncovering her Kojak-like cranium.

Inexplicably, my dreams have never featured me dangling Sister Agnes Marita upside down out the window, her bloomers exposed as her habit hung over her ears.

Instead, I dream of returning to school only to find myself in difficult situations. I'll walk into a classroom and be unable to find my seat while a nun hollers at me to be seated. In some dreams, I can't find my classroom. I repeatedly dream of returning to class in eighth grade, despite my college degree, to finish some test that remained incomplete over the decades. I'm an adult sitting in a child's chair and desk, trying to fulfill some long-overdue, academic obligation. The common denominator of all my Immaculate Conception dreams is, they all highlight stressful situations.

I'd prefer to dream of a nun walking across a busy intersection carrying a bag of groceries when

I come rumbling along in the driver's seat of a Humvee. I'd yell out the window, "I don't brake for nuns!" and hit the gas. With hands clenched on the steering wheel and lip snarled, I'd bear down on the black shrouded pedestrian like a locomotive about to sweep away a cow from its tracks.

If you take a good look around, in the cities, you will notice that you don't see nuns venturing out in the crosswalks. And for good reason. I'm not the only refugee from Catholic School who doesn't brake for nuns. There are legions of us.

Copyright © 2003-2010 Richard J. Phillips

About Rick Phillips

Rick is president of Phillips & Associates, a marketing company he started in 1982. He is an expert in the field of public relations and full-spectrum marketing, and his company specializes in census building for retirement and real estate communities nationwide.

Simultaneous to pursuing his marketing career, Rick has been a newspaper columnist, inventor and entrepreneurial product developer. He has also produced dozens of TV commercials, video brochures and has scripted several teleplays and series developments.

Rick is a graduate of University of Miami with a degree in Communications and Creative Writing. He also attended University of Southern California's renowned Cinema School.

Having worked his way through college at the Los Angeles Times and then the Miami Herald, Rick became a sports editor for Panax Newspapers. The Florida Press Club bestowed the award "General Excellence in Sportswriting" upon him in 1979.

Before embarking on his own business, Rick was the first public relations coordinator for the City of North Miami Beach, and later an Account Executive at a large Florida PR firm specializing in real estate development.